The Urbana Free Library

WASHINGTON, D.C., BY ROAD

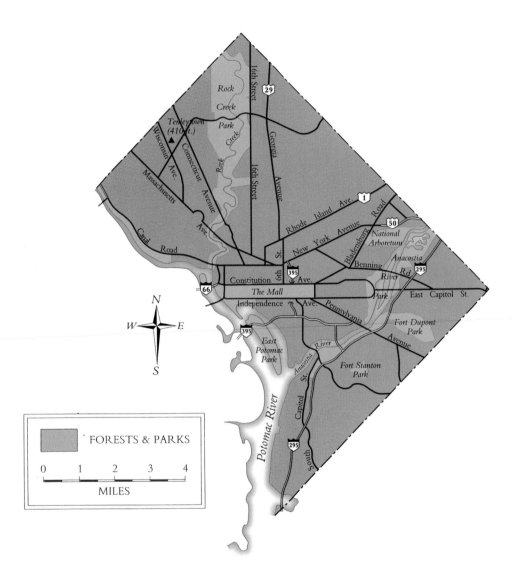

Celebrate the States

Washington, D.C.

Dan Elish

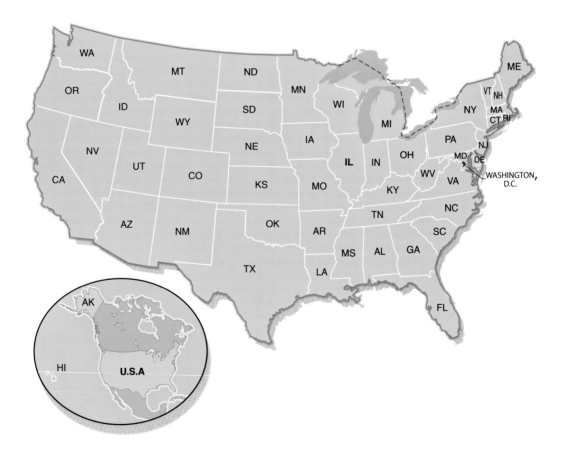

Marshall Cavendish
Benchmark
New York

Marshall Cavendish Benchmark
99 White Plains Road
Tarrytown, NY 10591-9001
www.marshallcavendish.us

Library of Congress Cataloging-in-Publication Data
Elish, Dan.
Washington, D.C. / by Dan Elish.—2nd ed.
p. cm. — (Celebrate the states)
Summary: "Provides comprehensive information on the geography, history, wildlife, governmental
structure, economy, cultural diversity, peoples, religion, and landmarks
of Washington, D.C."—Provided by publisher.
Includes bibliographical references and index.
ISBN-13: 978-0-7614-2352-2
ISBN-10: 0-7614-2352-4
1. Washington (D.C.)—Juvenile literature. I. Title. II. Series.
F194.3.E45 2007   975.3—dc22   2006013838

Editor: Christine Florie
Editorial Director: Michelle Bisson
Art Director: Anahid Hamparian
Series Designer: Adam Meitlowski

Photo research by Connie Gardner

Cover Photo: Bill Ross/CORBIS

The photographs in this book are used by permission and courtesy of: *Corbis:* Art Stein/zuma, 12;
Bettmann, 13, 41, 120; James P. Blair, 14; E. Sachse and Co., 26; Reuters, 42, 60; Layne Kennedy, 44;
Corbis, 46; Icon SMI, 59; Wally McNamee, 63; Ron Watts, 80; Andrew Cutraro/epa, 84; Gregg New-
ton, 90, 92; Josephm Sohm, 94, 105; Lester Lefkowitz, 96; Richard T. Nowitz, 97, 102, 107; Picture
Net, 101; Darrell Gulin, 115; Matthew Cavanaugh/epa, 122; Gregory Pace, 124; Murat Tanner/zefa,
131; Lee Snider/Photo Images, 133; *PhotoEdit:* Tom Carter, 52; Cleve Bryant, 76; Michael Ventura, 98;
David Young Wolff, 119; *Alamy:* Michael Matthews, 73; Mike McKavett, 109 (top); John G. Wilbanks,
113; *James Leynse:* 83; *Peter Arnold:* David Cavagnaro, 109 (bottom); Getty: National Geographic, back
cover; Alex Wong, 17; Stock Food Creative, 56; Aftp, 86; Hulton Archive, 128; *The Image Works:* Rob
Crandall, 8; Chet Gordon, 16; Joe Sohm, 20; Steven Rubin, 49; Andre Jenny, 64; Adam Tanner, 71;
Sven Martson, 103; Ann Ronan Picture Library, 123; Lebrecht, 125; *SuperStock:* Randy Santos, 11; Ping
Amranand, 54; Kurt Scholz, 57; Robert Liewellyn, 62; James Lemass, 136; *Bridgeman Art Library:* View
of the Capitol from the White House in 1840 (colored engraving) by Bartlett, William Henry (1809-54)
Peter Newark American Pictures; *The Granger Collection:* 25, 28, 29, 30, 31, 33, 34, 35; *AP Photo:*
Reginald Pearman, Stringer, 67; Haraz N. Ghanbari, 69; Rick Bowmer, 78.

Printed in China
1 3 5 6 4 2

Contents

Washington, D.C., is an exciting place to live.

"Everyone who is important in the world today has to eventually find themselves here."

—teacher Ann O'Connell

Since its birth Washington, D.C., has been a beacon to world travelers.

"It is sometimes called the City of Magnificent Distances, but it might with greater propriety be termed the City of Magnificent Intentions."

—writer Charles Dickens

Washington, D.C., is the home of the U.S. national government. Many admire its great politicians.

"It's a thrill to walk down Pennsylvania Avenue and realize that great men like Theodore Roosevelt and Woodrow Wilson walked there, too. This city has a wonderful sense of history."

—salesman Frank Bucking

Washington, D.C., is beautiful.

"I never lose the thrill of seeing the Capitol Building lit up at night."

—attorney Barbara Eyman

The annual Cherry Blossom Festival makes Washington "the most beautiful city in the world, at least for two weeks."

—D.C. delegate Eleanor Holmes Norton

For much of its history Washington, D.C., has been like two different cities: one for the wealthy, the other for the mostly black poor.

"This is the same city where the president of the United States lives and [the black community is] living in a war zone."

—community advocate Mike Johnson

Even though Washington, D.C., has been through some hard economic times, there is great reason to hope for the future.

"I never would have believed it. After years of mismanagement, Washington's budget has a surplus. Better still, the trash is actually picked up and, the last time it snowed, they plowed the streets right away."

—journalist Steve Harkin

Indeed, things in Washington, D.C., are looking up.

"Despite all its problems, Washington has so much potential. There's a great spirit here, a great energy, along with all those gorgeous monuments. This is where I want to be. This is where it's all happening."

—student Phyllis Hall

Washington, D.C., is a city of grandeur and majesty. It is next to impossible to walk along its famous Mall and not feel the power of our country's great history. The words of the timeless Gettysburg Address adorning the Lincoln Memorial or the thousands of names of lost soldiers carved into the black granite of the Vietnam Veterans Memorial are stirring testaments to our nation's past.

Historically, there has always been another side to Washington, beyond the proud monuments, the White House, and Congress. Through many years of mismanagement and money shortages, the city struggled for its economic survival. But over the past decade Washington has taken significant steps to change that. Today, housing values are shooting up, services are drastically improved, and the city has a balanced budget. Of course, there is still work to be done. Crime is still a problem. Public schools are still poor. Even so, today's Washingtonians can feel proud that life in the capital city is improving by leaps and bounds.

Chapter One

The Nation's Capital

When most American citizens think of our nation's capital, they imagine the White House, marble monuments, and the dome of the Capitol. They picture members of the Senate hurrying to the Senate floor to cast a vote or the president in the Oval Office working on an important speech. What most people don't know is that when Congress agreed on the general location for the capital city in 1790, Washington, D.C., was what Thomas Jefferson, the author of the Declaration of Independence and our country's third president, called "an Indian swamp in the wilderness." Indeed, the Washington of yesteryear was densely wooded, with numerous creeks and springs. Cows, pigs, and sheep roamed freely through the dirt streets. There were few stores and homes.

It took many years and much hard work to turn that swampy land into one of the world's most stunning cities. Located in a 68-square-mile nook between Maryland and Virginia, Washington is the capital of the world's only remaining superpower. Though its population is only 550,521 people, it is the home of senators, representatives, and diplomats from all over the globe. Virtually every critical world issue is debated in this city on the banks

Washington, D.C., is an urban center with monuments and government buildings that symbolize the culture and history of the nation's capital.

of the Potomac River. One resident remarked, "Every day on the way to work, a thought lurks in the back of my mind: that the president works down the block. And the vice president, too. Not to mention Congress. What can I say? It may sound corny, but I find that very exciting. Washington is the center of not only our country but of the world."

GETTING AROUND WASHINGTON

It was George Washington himself who hand-picked Pierre-Charles L'Enfant, a brilliant French engineer, artist, and architect he had met at Valley Forge during the Revolutionary War, to be the planner of the city that would bear his name. But if you mention the name L'Enfant to a Washingtonian today, the famed Frenchman is liable to get mixed reviews.

"In theory," said Michael Richards, a D.C. lawyer, "Washington was set up by L'Enfant to be easy to get around. In practice, though, unless you've lived here for a while, it's nearly impossible to know where you are."

Of course, it is not really fair to blame L'Enfant for how Washington works today. As the writer Leslie Pillner put it, "It's hard to know whether it was L'Enfant's fault or if everybody who has come since messed up his plan."

The debate will undoubtedly continue for years to come. It is certainly true that L'Enfant's original concept had its merits. L'Enfant imagined a grand city, worthy of a proud new nation, divided into four sections—the Northwest, Northeast, Southwest, and Southeast—with the Capitol at its center. Two hundred years later, that's exactly how the city is divided. The streets are numbered to the north and south and lettered to the east and west. Though this seems straightforward on paper, as Washington has grown, the system has gone somewhat awry. "Streets appear, then disappear, then appear again," one longtime resident said. "It's frustrating."

Complicating things further are the traffic circles located throughout the city. They were originally designed by L'Enfant as defensive emplacements where soldiers armed with cannons could stop invaders. But now, Michael Richards said, "All they succeed in doing is confusing people." A street reaches a traffic circle on one side and then disappears on the other.

Many natives prefer to get around town on the clean and efficient Metro, one of the world's most impressive subway systems. Unlike the city streets, the Metro's maps are extremely clear and easy to follow.

Washington, D.C., is the only major city in the United States that was planned.

THE METRO

"The D.C. Metro is one of the wonders of the Western World," said the reporter Frank Clines. "It's still as pristine now as it was when it opened."

Most Washingtonians would agree. The D.C. system is one of the most safe, efficient, and reliable—not to mention clean and comfortable—subways in America. Trains are constructed from graffiti-resistant materials, and maps are easy to follow. Built deep underground because of Washington's swampy terrain, most Metro stops are entered through long escalators that can be almost as fun to ride as the train itself!

As today's city pushes out to the suburbs, new Metro stops are being planned. One of the most ambitious is a 23-mile-long line from Falls Church, Virginia, through what was once farmland, to Washington Dulles International Airport in Dulles, Virginia. Land next to Metro stops is being developed into housing designed to appeal to young professionals.

Indeed, the Metro stands as a shining success in a city that still has a reputation for poor public services. One resident said, "We may have our problems right now compared to some other cities, but this is one thing we've got over everyone!"

Many know that our nation's capital is home to the Washington Monument, the 555-foot-tall white marble obelisk built to honor George Washington. What many people don't know is that it is the tallest building in Washington, thanks to a 1910 law that restricts the height of structures to no more than the width of the street it is on. "There's a great feeling of openness," noted Leslie DeCrette, a tourist. "It's an altogether different feeling than New York or Chicago, where everything is so built up." "Washington has no skyscrapers blocking the sunlight," said Rick McAllister, a teacher. "It's refreshing in a major city."

All of that sunlight shines onto Pierre-Charles L'Enfant's wide avenues, many of which are graced by majestic trees, including "exotics"—Oriental ginkgoes, ailanthus, and Asiatic magnolias—imported to America from other countries. In 1805 President Jefferson did what he could to beautify the city by authorizing the planting of Lombardy poplars along Pennsylvania Avenue. In the early 1870s the Board of Public Works, an agency dominated by one of its members, Alexander Robey "Boss" Shepherd, planted many trees. In the mid-1960s Lady Bird Johnson, the wife of President Lyndon Johnson, made the beautification of D.C. a top priority.

The tallest structure in the Washington, D.C., skyline is the Washington Monument.

The U.S. National Arboretum was established in 1927 by Congress. Its mission is to educate the public and to conduct scientific research.

It is partly a result of her efforts that Washington is home to 150 parks, where such flowers as tulips, daffodils, and azaleas bloom. The district also supports a fair amount of wildlife. In residential areas deer, raccoons, foxes, and opossums flourish. In the spring the bright songs of migrating warblers, thrushes, and finches fill the park.

Obviously, the most striking feature of the nation's capital is not its nature. What Washington is justifiably famous for are its noble monuments, magnificent museums, and stately architecture. Washington is home to the Mall, one of the most gorgeous pieces of real estate in the country. Within walking distance lie the Lincoln Memorial, the Jefferson Memorial, the Capitol, and the Washington Monument.

"But what I like best about this city," said one resident, "are the less famous spots. Have you ever walked down Massachusetts Avenue past Embassy Row? It sounds corny, but it's a thrill to see all those stately buildings with guards out front, with the countries' flags flapping in the breeze."

CLIMATE

"Washington's climate? Heat, heat, and more heat. And don't get me started on the humidity! That's the weather in the nation's capital from May to September," said one native.

Indeed, in the summer Washington is an extremely humid town with long heat waves during which temperatures reach into the nineties, which make its residents thankful for air-conditioning. "July and August are particularly terrible," one government employee noted. But at least it's not as bad as the city's earlier days. In the nineteenth century the summer brought malaria and yellow fever epidemics as the sun pounded the mosquito-infested marshes.

The summer months can be hot and humid in Washington, D.C. These visitors cool off in the fountain in the sculpture garden at the National Gallery of Art.

Winter in the district can be a mixed bag of cold days followed by warm ones. When nor'easters, windy storms on the East Coast, blow in, it's cold and wet. When the warm air from Bermuda waltzes through, it's windbreaker weather. Southerners at heart, most Washingtonians have trouble adapting to the occasional snowstorm. Schools shut down, and people stay home from work in droves even if there's snow in the forecast, let alone an inch or two on the ground.

Fall brings beautiful colors to Washington's many trees, but most residents agree that spring is the nicest time of year in the nation's capital. According to Michael Richards, "Spring is marvelous—and long. It tiptoes in in late February and lasts until mid-May. While Bostonians are still in down jackets and New Yorkers are getting chestnuts roasted on an open fire, D.C.'s weather is splendid."

Skiing through Washington, D.C., is one way of getting around during a snow storm.

ENVIRONMENTAL CONCERNS

One of the great challenges that faces any city is protecting the environment. In the past the inefficiency of Washington's government sometimes contributed to its environmental problems. In the summer of 1996 Washington residents were told to boil their drinking water. Years of neglect had allowed lead and dangerous bacteria to seep into the water supply, a problem that was solved when the city added chlorine to the drinking water. Likewise, in the late 1990s the city was forced to suspend curbside recycling due to a lack of funds. Thankfully, a few years later the district found the money to reinstate the program.

Like many metropolitan areas around the world, Washington has struggled with finding a solution to the problem of air pollution, specifically car exhaust. In the 1990s the number of Washingtonians who drove to work increased by a quarter of a million people. Worse, the number of passengers per car has been estimated at 1.13. On top of that, government agencies offer free parking to many of their workers, giving commuters little incentive to leave their cars at home. "For work, there's no question, that's my incentive to drive," said Jim Forbes, a press officer for Congress. "If I didn't have that [parking] space, I'd be on the Metro."

Though some organizations have proposed imposing a $1 parking fee to encourage drivers to carpool or take the bus, no law has been passed. That doesn't mean the government isn't doing anything about air pollution in the district. In 2005 the city council passed a regulation that states that vehicles must not idle for more than three minutes while parked. The only exceptions are when it is cold outside or when there are more than twelve people on a bus with air-conditioning.

"Every little bit helps," said the longtime Washington resident Peter Allen. "But the more people carpool, the better the air is going to be."

TROUBLE ON KLINGLE ROAD

Klingle Road runs through Washington's beautiful Rock Creek Park. For years it was open to traffic, allowing Washingtonians to get around the city while admiring the park's natural beauty. In 1991 it was deemed impassable and closed. Today, Washingtonians who live near it are arguing passionately over whether to open it back up to cars. "It's simple," said John Rogers, an architect. "Bringing back cars will wreck the landscape and pollute the creek. It's pointless." Obviously, there are those who disagree. "Traffic is Washington's number-one problem," said a resident. "[Getting] any other roads to help us get around this city is a good thing."

The disagreement over Klingle Road reflects people's views on the importance of preserving the environment. It also exposes some of the class differences that exist in any city. While the wealthier people west of Rock Creek Park don't want people commuting through their neighborhoods, the poorer citizens in the east want the road to open. "This fight has been going on for years now," said one D.C. resident. "And I don't think it's going to end anytime soon."

The Anacostia River

In the 1970s a major cleanup effort transformed the once-dirty Potomac River into a beautiful waterway. Today, the city's focus is on the district's "Forgotten River," the Anacostia, a waterway that wends its way through the heart of the nation's capital for 8 miles. Though surrounded by parkland, the Anacostia is horribly polluted. "Part of the problem is that the

The Potomac Riverkeeper is an organization that works to protect and restore the Potomac River through education and citizen involvement.

Anacostia moves really, really slowly," said Irene Gumm, a teacher. "So the river doesn't flush the pollutants out."

Another problem is urban development. From the late nineteenth century through the present day, forest and wetlands were destroyed to control insects and to make way for homes. More buildings mean more pavement. When it rains, storm water that used to soak into the ground now picks up pollutants and runs directly into the river. Washington also collects storm water and some sewage in the same pipes. After a rainstorm, the pipes often become overwhelmed and dump untreated sewage into the river as well.

Recently, environmentally concerned Washingtonians decided it was time to get serious about cleaning up the Anacostia. Groups are replacing open land so that rainwater will soak into the earth instead of flowing into the sewers and the river. Regulations are being rewritten so that storm water and sewage will use different pipes. This will reduce the chances of sewage overflowing into the river. "The federal government has a part to play, too," said longtime Washington resident Phyllis Hall. "They own most of the land in this city and have the most bathrooms." In truth, federal buildings account for 18 percent of the sewage runoff that ends up in the river.

Perhaps most important, Mayor Anthony A. Williams made the cleanup of the district's forgotten river a priority. In March 2000 he began the Anacostia Waterfront Initiative, an effort that would not only clean up the river but would also fill the surrounding land with parks, pedestrian and bike paths, and revitalized neighborhoods.

The manager of the project, Uwe Brandes, put it like this: "Rivers can play an important role in the regeneration of cities. Historically, they've been seen as a way to dump pollution. Now, the national resurgence of the river itself can be the green engine of growth."

Chapter Two

Gateway to History

"History is rich in Washington," said the painter Suzanne O'Neill. "You breathe it in every time you walk outside." Indeed, it is nearly impossible to walk around downtown Washington and not run into a monument to our nation's past. Living in Washington, you might work near the National Archives where the Declaration of Independence is kept on display. Or perhaps you would have a business meeting near the White House.

Though Washington is an American city that has borne witness to our nation's highest and lowest moments, the district also has a local history. It is a history of the people who lived in Washington long before Thomas Jefferson or Alexander Hamilton were born and a history of ordinary people who came to Washington in search of a better life.

EARLY SETTLERS

Archaeologists believe the area that is now Washington, D.C., has been inhabited for around 13,000 years. Paleo-Indians lived in the area from 11,000 to 8000 B.C.E. These Native Americans were hunter-gatherers who

William Henry Bartlett was an English painter who visited the United States four times between 1836 and 1852. On his trip in 1840 he painted the view of the Capitol from the White House.

lived in small tribes and gathered nuts and berries. Some archaeologists believe that the Paleo-Indians also hunted and contributed to the decline of big game animals, such as caribou, elk, and moose.

The Archaic Period (8000–2000 B.C.E.) saw great changes in Washington's landscape. The climate became warmer, melting glaciers and flooding rivers. The Chesapeake Bay was formed. During this time native populations grew and began to hunt smaller game. An increase in plant life and game allowed tribes to settle in one place and set up permanent communities. These ancient men and women made such basic tools as axes and bowls.

During the Woodland Period (100 B.C.E.–C.E. 1600) natives used the land that is present-day Rock Creek Park as hunting and fishing grounds. The people lived in wigwams, one-room structures made of bent saplings covered with bark, grass, and reeds. A fire burned in the center of a wigwam during winter for warmth. By C.E. 600 tribes of Native Americans lived across the East Coast of present day America. A series of footpaths connected their villages, and trade routes ran all the way to the Ohio Valley.

THE PISCATAWAY AND THE COMING OF THE EUROPEANS

By the early 1600s the dominant tribe in the Washington area was the Piscataway, who resided in villages surrounded by stake fences. They raised corn, squash, and other vegetables and fished the Potomac and Anacostia rivers.

Though the Piscataway were peaceful, they were kept busy trying to steer clear of the warlike Iroquois, who lived to the north. In the early 1600s, when British colonists first appeared in Maryland and Virginia, the Piscataway tried to form alliances with the newcomers. Instead, the natives fell victim to smallpox, commonly known as "white man's disease." By 1680 most of the Piscataway had moved

Iroquois villages were surrounded by palisades, tall, sharpened logs embedded in the ground to protect the village from enemies. Inside, longhouses were built that held a large number of people.

north and had been absorbed into various Iroquois tribes. Though the Iroquois survived for many more years, they too were ultimately overrun by the Europeans.

In 1634 the land that is now the District of Columbia became part of Britain's Maryland Colony. Back then, most of Maryland was devoted to growing tobacco and was divided into large plantations that were worked by slaves. The first plantation within present-day Washington,

Duddington Manor, was established in 1664. Life was very good for the rich plantation owners. While slaves did most of the work in the fields, the masters enjoyed horse races, fencing, and a calendar full of parties.

In 1751 the first of Washington's present-day neighborhoods was founded when Marylanders established Georgetown, named after King George II of England. Georgetown soon became a thriving port.

Georgetown grew to be a profitable town upon its tobacco trade and its successful shipping port.

On July 4, 1776, the Continental Congress signed Thomas Jefferson's Declaration of Independence, a document that laid out the American colonies' grievances against the British Empire. In the course of the hard-fought Revolutionary War that followed, General George Washington became a national hero. Eventually, the Constitution was written, and Washington was elected first president of the United States.

But there was one minor problem—where to put the capital? Though Philadelphia had served as the temporary capital, Congress had also met in New York City; Baltimore and Annapolis, Maryland; Trenton, New Jersey; and York, Pennsylvania. Of course, nearly every city in the country wanted to be the nation's capital. After all, the mayors and citizens of each town correctly assumed that the nation's new capital would attract commerce and therefore money. It was an important and difficult decision. Finally, one congressman said, "We will make enemies no matter which city we choose. So let us build a completely new town for our national capital." The nation's founders recognized the historic opportunity that lay before them. Pierre-Charles L'Enfant wrote to George Washington, "No nation, perhaps, had ever before been offered the opportunity of deliberately deciding on the spot where their capital should be fixed."

But that choice was not easy. Though the United States did not fight the Civil War until 1861, the young country was already brimming with tensions between the North and South. Thomas Jefferson, President Washington's secretary of state, was from Virginia and felt that the capital should be near his home state. George Washington, also from Virginia, wanted a capital near his home at Mount Vernon in Virginia. But many northerners objected. Finally, Jefferson struck a deal with Alexander Hamilton, a northerner who headed the Treasury Department.

Hamilton was worried about the nation's heavy war debts. Though the Revolutionary War had given the nation its cherished freedom, it had also cost a lot of money. Jefferson agreed to use his influence to persuade Congress to put up the cash to pay off the war debts, and in return Hamilton supported a site on the Potomac River for the new capital. George Washington was given the honor of choosing the exact spot, which he announced in 1791.

So the location of present-day Washington was picked. After Maryland and Virginia ceded control over the land to create the capital, George Washington asked the nineteen property owners in the new Washington city to give the federal government enough land to build the city's streets. He also asked if they would sell the government enough land for the president's home, a capitol, and various federal buildings at $66.66 an acre. The owners agreed, believing that the property values of the land they held onto would skyrocket when the district became a thriving city. With the land secured, President Washington got in touch with Pierre-Charles L'Enfant.

This fresco by Allyn Cox depicts George Washington and Pierre-Charles L'Enfant choosing the site of the capital.

THE FOUNDING FATHER

It is ironic that the man who gave his name to his country's capital never actually lived there. When George Washington became president in 1789, New York was the nation's capital, and he and the first lady, Martha, lived in what is now lower Manhattan. But even though Washington never actually lived in the city that bears his name, it was the honor with which he carried himself as the first president that gave the nation's new government legitimacy. George Washington was the steady, firm leader to whom all could turn. When he wanted to step down from the presidency after his first term in office, two bitter rivals, Thomas Jefferson, then secretary of state, and Alexander Hamilton, the secretary of the treasury, begged him to remain. By the time he did retire in 1797, he had successfully guided the United States through a rocky start. The experimental stage of the country was over, and the presidency could be turned over to someone else.

Like many Frenchmen of his day, Pierre-Charles L'Enfant, an architect and a military engineer, had volunteered to fight on the side of the American rebels during the Revolutionary War. L'Enfant became a member of General George Washington's staff. After the war L'Enfant worked as an architect and engineer in New York. (L'Enfant was also responsible for designing the Purple Heart, a medal awarded to wounded American soldiers.) When he heard about the new capital, he immediately dashed off a letter to General Washington, asking if he could take part in the planning.

French engineer Pierre-Charles L'Enfant designed the federal capital for George Washington.

Washington was impressed by his enthusiasm. L'Enfant arrived in the city in 1791, eager to get to work.

With the assistance of Andrew Ellicott, a surveyor from Pennsylvania, and his assistant, Benjamin Banneker, an African-American astronomer and mathematician, L'Enfant traveled the countryside surveying the land. Three weeks later he made public his plan for a city full of monuments, a presidential palace, a statue of George Washington, and, at the very center on a spot called Jenkins Hill, the Capitol. Connecting the Capitol and the president's home would be a ceremonial boulevard (today's Pennsylvania Avenue). Extending westward from the Capitol would be a "vast esplanade" (today's Mall, home of the Smithsonian museums and various monuments).

L'Enfant's plans seemed too ambitious for most Washingtonians. His call for broad streets, 100 to 110 feet wide, infuriated the landowners who had been persuaded to give up their property at a low price.

Congress adopted Andrew Ellicott's map, based upon Pierre-Charles L'Enfant's plans for the federal city of Washington.

(Most infuriating was Pennsylvania Avenue, which was to be 400 feet wide!) L'Enfant also proved uncompromising. Once he committed his ideas to paper, he refused to change them. The last straw came when Daniel Carroll, heir to Duddington Manor, began constructing a house that would block one of the Frenchman's planned avenues. In a fit of rage L'Enfant ordered the house torn down. There was nothing George Washington could do but relieve the talented architect of his duties. Though Congress offered him $2,500 for his efforts (no small sum in those days), the furious L'Enfant refused. The Frenchman's plans were still used, however, with minor modifications. Having never received a single cent for all his hard work, L'Enfant died in poverty in 1825.

THE NEW CAPITAL

While the new capital was being developed, the federal government remained in Philadelphia. In late 1800 it finally moved to Washington. Today, Washington and Philadelphia are connected by highways. In 1800 the area between the two cities was mostly forest and mosquito-infested swamps.

In November of 1800 First Lady Abigail Adams made the trip from Philadelphia to Washington. She arrived in Baltimore with no major mishaps. But shortly after leaving Baltimore for Washington, her carriage took a wrong turn, and her party was forced to hack its way through thick woods to get back to the road that connected the two cities. She later wrote to her sister, "You find nothing by a forest and woods on the way; for 16 and 18 miles not a village."

Like Abigail Adams, the rest of the nation's government made their slow way to the new capital city. Luckily, Washington was not yet burdened by excessive bureaucracy. In 1802 the young country employed only 291 people.

The Washington of the early 1800s was not nearly as magnificent as the Washington of today. There was only one recognizable street, today's New Jersey Avenue. Pennsylvania Avenue did not yet exist. Instead, the space between the president's house and Congress was covered with alder bushes. Cows grazed by the uncompleted streets, hogs ran in the mud, and cornfields grew by homes. One visiting New Yorker remarked, "We only need more houses, cellars, kitchens, scholarly men, amiable women, and a few other such trifles to possess a perfect city."

BUILDING THE WHITE HOUSE

When Congress established the District of Columbia on July 16, 1790, a competition was held for the honor of designing the White House. An Irishman named James Hoban won with a design modeled after a palace in Dublin, Ireland. Construction began on October 13, 1792. Most of the laborers who worked on the building were African American, both enslaved and free. Unfortunately, construction took too long for George Washington to have a chance to live there. The president's home was finally completed on November 1, 1800. The first president to move in was John Adams.

For the first decade of the 1800s the mansion was called the Presidential Palace. Around 1811 the public had come to call the home by its color, the White House.

THE WAR OF 1812

The early 1800s were marked by tension between the young nation and Europe. With Britain and France at war, President Thomas Jefferson tried to keep the United States neutral. To stop the United States from trading with France, British ships began to board American ships on the high seas and impress, or force, American sailors to join the British navy. At the same time some Americans were eager to grab British land in the west.

By 1812 it became clear that Britain was not going to stop interfering with America's ships, and President James Madison declared war.

The burning of Washington, D.C., by the British in 1814 destroyed public buildings, including the White House.

When the War of 1812 began, Washington was still a half-built city. The powerful British navy easily overwhelmed American ships, and on August 24, 1814, British troops invaded Washington, torching the White House and many other unfinished public buildings. The Americans fought back. When both sides finally conceded that the war had reached a stalemate, hostilities were brought to a close with the signing of the Treaty of Ghent in 1815. With the war over, the nation had to start from scratch and rebuild Washington from the rubble.

THE CIVIL WAR

Though Washington's population increased from 14,000 in 1800 to around 35,000 by 1832, Americans were hardly flocking to the hot and humid city. Much of Washington was still largely undeveloped, and disease-carrying mosquitoes were a serious problem along the riverbanks. L'Enfant's wide avenues remained unfinished. After seeing the Capitol in 1828, one English writer noted, "Everybody knows that Washington has a Capitol, but the misfortune is that the Capitol wants a city. There it stands, reminding you of a general without an army, only surrounded and followed by a parcel of ragged little boys, for such is the appearance of the dirty, straggling, ill-built houses which lie at the foot of it."

The residents of those "ill-built" houses were more often than not the 11,000 free African-American men and women who by 1860 had migrated from the South and worked in largely menial jobs. Washington also allowed slavery. In fact, the city was a center for the slave trade, causing one man to observe, "You call this the land of liberty, and every day things are done in it at which the despotisms of Europe would be horror-struck and disgusted. . . . In no part of the earth . . . is there so great, so infamous a slave market, as in the metropolis, in the seat of government of this nation which prides itself on freedom."

Indeed, slavery was one of the issues that drove Americans to the Civil War, a conflict that had an enormous effect on Washington. During the war the city became the major supply depot and hospital camp for the Union army. Food and water ran low. Typhoid and dysentery epidemics ravaged the town. Hundreds of private homes, churches, and warehouses were used as army barracks and hospitals.

When the exhausting war was finally won by the North in 1865, Washington was in shambles. Washington's population had risen to 100,000, overwhelming the city. Poor people, many of them newly freed slaves, migrated from the South and settled in shacks. These new citizens had been agricultural workers and had few skills to use in a town where the government was the main employer.

Located between upper and lower southern states, Washington, D.C., was a major slave trade center.

WE'LL FIGHT FOR UNCLE ABE

The song *We'll Fight for Uncle Abe* praises Civil War generals Ulysses S. Grant and George Brinton McClellan, while expressing the growing popularity of "Uncle Abe" Lincoln. Although the actual fighting had been taking place in Virginia and points farther south, it was Washington, D.C., that symbolized the Union's struggle against the Confederacy.

Words by C. E. Pratt
Music by Frederick Buckley

Way down in old Var-gin-ny, I sup-pose you all do know, They have tried to bust the Un-ion, But they find it is no go. The Yan-kee boys are start-ing out, The Un-ion for to save, And we're go-ing down to Wash-ing-ton To fight for Un-cle Abe.

Rip, Rap, Flip, Flap, Strap your knap - sack on your back, For we're goin' down to Wash - ing - ton to fight for Un - cle Abe.

There is General Grant at Vicksburg,
Just see what he has done,
He has taken sixty cannon
And made the Rebels run,
And next he will take Richmond,
I'll bet you half a dollar,
And if he catches General Johnson,
Oh won't he make him holler. *Chorus*

The season now is coming
When the roads begin to dry;
Soon the Army of the Potomac
Will make the Rebels fly,
For General McClellan, he's the man,
The Union for to save;
Oh! Hail Columbia's right side up,
And so's your Uncle Abe. *Chorus*

You may talk of Southern chivalry
And cotton being king,
But I guess before the war is done
You'll think another thing;
They say that recognition
Will the Rebel country save,
But Johnny Bull and Mister France
Are 'fraid of Uncle Abe. *Chorus*

In 1870 a plumber and local politician named Alexander Shepherd was appointed to Washington's Board of Public Works. Drawing on funds allocated by Congress, Shepherd organized crews of poor workers, to pave roads, plant trees, and dig sewers. As the city gradually became more livable, it attracted foreign investment. But Shepherd spent more money than he had been allotted and left the city $18 million in debt. At the same time the Fifteenth Amendment had given African Americans the right to vote. After the war formerly enslaved African Americans poured into the district and began to influence local politics. Whites from Maryland and Virginia didn't like it and lobbied Congress to take away the voting rights of every Washingtonian in order to stop newly free African Americans from gaining too much power. As a result, in 1874 Congress put the city under the auspices of three commissioners appointed by the president. Just like that, all Washington citizens lost the right to vote. The capital of the "land of the free" was ruled by Congress like a colony.

In the years leading up to the twentieth century the government that expanded during the Civil War remained large. As always, the federal government remained the city's main employer, providing jobs and fueling economic growth.

FACING THE TWENTIETH CENTURY

World War I affected Washington in much the same way as the Civil War had—the population rose dramatically, this time to 450,000, and shortages again struck the city. The 1920s brought a building boom (many monuments were completed, including the Lincoln Memorial in 1922), and the Great Depression of the 1930s caused President Franklin Roosevelt to initiate a program he called the New Deal, which created thousands of

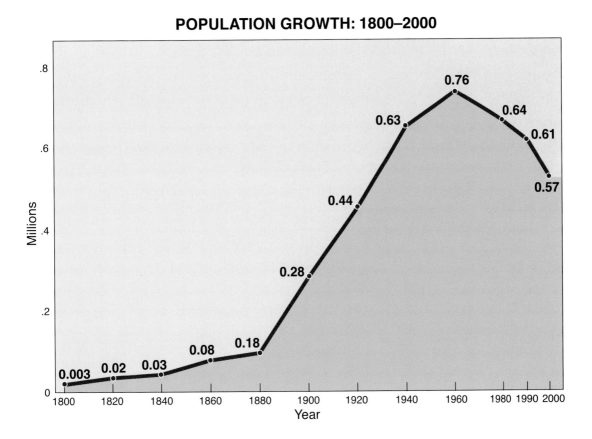

POPULATION GROWTH: 1800–2000

government jobs for out-of-work Americans and expanded the size of the Washington bureaucracy and population yet again.

As the United States entered World War II in 1941, many Washingtonians, mostly African American, still lived in poor conditions. In 1944 Senator Theodore Bilbo became chairman of the Senate District Committee that oversaw Washington. Bilbo was a virulent segregationist who once opposed an antilynching law and proposed a bill that would have deported twelve million blacks to Liberia. Though known as "the Mayor of Washington," Bilbo was so racist that he did whatever he could to deny the district funds. Black Washingtonians did not thrive with Theodore Bilbo in charge.

In the 1950s, after Bilbo's death, Washington's District Committee was taken over by another white segregationist, John L. McMillan of South Carolina. Not much better than his predecessor, "Johnny Mack" refused to even hold hearings on various proposals for Washington's self-government. Thus, into the 1960s Congress continued to run Washington without much thought for the welfare of its citizens. As one journalist put it, "Today's speeches about the glories of democracy should always be followed by the words 'except in Washington.' The fact that those who live in the seat of democracy do not enjoy its basic prerogatives is quite literally incredible." In other words, Washingtonians endured "taxation without representation."

HOME RULE AT LAST

Since the end of home rule, or self-government, in 1874, Washingtonians had struggled to get back their basic rights. In 1965 President Lyndon Johnson fought to give the citizens of Washington home rule but was voted down by the same vocal minority of southern segregationists who had always stood in the way.

But after the riots following the assassination of Dr. Martin Luther King Jr., the climate changed. Congress's segregationists were gone. Coalitions of black and white Washingtonians worked with the White House to get justice. In 1970 Washingtonians regained the right to elect a delegate to the House of Representatives. In 1973 Congress gave Washington the right to elect its own mayor, an act that was approved by district residents a year later. Finally, the district had won home rule. Though Congress still held veto power over Washington, D.C., legislation and approved the budget, the people of the district had the right to make some decisions for themselves.

THE RIOTS OF 1968

When the great civil rights leader Rev. Dr. Martin Luther King Jr. was assassinated in April 1968, anger in African-American communities across America boiled over. In Washington, for three horrible days, up to 20,000 people broke windows, looted stores, and set fires, causing President Lyndon Johnson to call in federal troops. But even the presence of the army couldn't contain the rioters, and store after store was destroyed.

By the time it was over, 6,300 people had been arrested, and 12 had died. The value of the lost property was estimated at $15 million. Businesses that had sustained many African-American neighborhoods for years had been destroyed. The riots caused many middle-class people to move out of the city altogether.

The 1968 riots are still a dividing point in the city's history. People talk about the city "before the riots" and "after the riots." One African-American woman said, "It was a defining moment in my life. Before Dr. King's death, I had a feeling that things were going to work, people would get along, racism was under control. Then I realized it wasn't going to work."

THE PENATGON

On September 11, 2001, the Washington area was the target of a terror-
ist attack. On the same morning that two planes crashed into New York
City's World Trade Center, a hijacked plane crashed into the Pentagon,
the enormous building that is the headquarters of the U.S. Department
of Defense. The crash killed 125 people on the ground, along with 64
who were on the plane. Like all Americans, the people of Washington
quickly rallied. "It was nice to see the way the people of the city pulled
together," said the writer Leslie Pillner.

Contractors got to work renovating the Pentagon, an effort dubbed
the Phoenix Project. Part of the rebuilding included adding extra security measures to keep the people within the Pentagon safe in case of future
attacks. All in all the rebuilding effort was a success. The workers whose
offices had been damaged in the September 11 attacks began moving
back in on August 15, 2002—a month ahead of schedule.

LOOKING UP

In the mid-1990s the district went so deeply in debt that a congressional control board was established to oversee the city's finances. Happily, the days of fiscal mismanagement appear to be a thing of the past. Much of the credit belongs to Mayor Anthony A. Williams. Serving from 1999 to 2007, Williams instituted policies aimed at attracting new businesses, building new housing, and improving city services. Like any city, Washington still has work to do. Further, its difficult relationship with the federal government continues. Though the control board was disbanded in the late 1990s, the city still lives under the watchful eye of Congress, which continues to have the right to approve its budget and veto its laws.

Even so, the district is most definitely on the upswing. In 2005 Mayor Williams made a startling announcement. After years of being in the red, something amazing had occurred—the city had balanced its budget!

Chapter Three

Tale of Two Cities

Historically, our nation's capital has been one of the most racially divided cities in the country. Although it was the first American city with an African-American majority (according to the 1960 census), Washington has been accurately referred to as "the last colony," because its government was firmly controlled by a white, often segregationist, Congress. To this day any understanding of the nation's capital must include an understanding of long-term resentments between the majority African-American population and the minority white population who, for so many years, held the power in the city.

RACISM IN THE NATION'S CAPITAL

In 1890 a tall plantation owner and U.S. senator named John Tyler explained why Washingtonians had lost the right to vote: "The historical fact is simply this. That the Negroes came into this District from Virginia and Maryland and from other places . . . and they took possession of a certain part of the political power of this District . . . and there was but one way to get out—so Congress thought . . . and that was to deny the right of suffrage

Washington, D.C., is a diverse city, with strong African-American culture and heritage.

45

[the vote] entirely to every human being in the District and have every office here controlled by appointment instead of by election . . . in order to get rid of this load of Negro suffrage that was flooded in upon them."

Senator Tyler's words sum up the problems African Americans in Washington, D.C., faced for years. The city was under the thumb of southern senators and representatives who dominated the committee that controlled the city—people who were unsympathetic to the plight of the African-American citizenry. As more and more African Americans migrated north to the district during the Great Migration, the conditions in which they lived deteriorated. The influential African-American leader Malcolm X visited the city and observed, "I was astounded to find in the nation's capital, just a few blocks from Capitol Hill, thousands of Negroes living . . . in dirt-floor shacks along unspeakably filthy lanes with names like Pig Alley and Goat Alley." He also noted, "I saw other Negroes better off; they lived in blocks of

An African-American family in a poor section of Washington D.C., in 1937.

rundown red brick houses. The old 'Colonial' railroaders had told me about Washington having a lot of 'middle class' Negroes . . . who were working as laborers, janitors, porters, guards, taxi-drivers, and the like. For the Negro in Washington, mail carrying was a prestige job."

Indeed, these middle-class families had always been an enormous source of pride among Washington's African Americans. How upsetting, then, to be deprived of the basic rights to vote and to have congressional representation that every other American citizen enjoyed. That resentment built up over years and years of mistreatment by congressional committees, which used the district as a means to grant patronage jobs.

When the city won home rule in 1974, many African Americans were thrilled to finally have control in the first black-majority city, affectionately dubbed Chocolate City after a 1940s song that claimed, "Hey, we didn't get our 40 acres and a mule, but we did get you, Chocolate City. You don't need the bullet when you've got the ballot." But Washington's stubborn social problems have rubbed salt in the wounds of racial issues that, in a better world, would have quietly gone away years ago.

When the control board effectively took over the district's local government in 1995, many white Washingtonians were happy that steps were being taken to confront the city's fiscal woes. But many African Americans were not pleased. They viewed the control board as a means for whites to regain control of the city. Indeed, any issue in Washington has to be handled with the utmost sensitivity with regard to race. As Representative Thomas M. Davis of Virginia put it, "The difficulty has been every time Congress tried to intervene [in the affairs of the city], people yell home rule or racism." The lack of understanding between whites and blacks was typified in a T-shirt that found its way onto the backs of many young African Americans in the early 1990s: "It's a black thing; you wouldn't understand."

For years Washington has been home to a thriving African-American middle class. But beginning in the 1980s nearly 50,000 better-off African-American Washingtonians moved out of the district, many to the suburbs. Why have these middle-class blacks decided to put down roots elsewhere? Mostly for the better quality of life the suburbs provide, especially better public schools. A resident of Mount Rainier, one of the new black suburbs, said, "I wouldn't come back into the city because of all the problems that have cropped up since I left, basically the poor city services. I love Mount Rainier. It's like a little town with a mayor you can call up and who will come over on his bike."

Despite their preference for a more comfortable suburban life, many African Americans feel guilty that they have abandoned their city. Lucenia Dunn moved from Washington to Woodmere, a predominately African-American development, in 1989. "We were first proud of the Chocolate City," she said, "and it's hard to unloosen that level of loyalty to the concept of having a successful African-American-owned and operated and run city."

Maryland's Prince George's County has become one of the largest African-American suburbs in the country. Ironically, some of the county's richer African-American citizens have begun to worry about their home becoming a haven for the city's poorer blacks. As one resident noted, "People have moved here away from crime to good schools, and it's very clear that some don't want ghetto kids in their school buildings." Alvin Thorton, a school board member, agreed that "Some middle-class black people have the same prejudices as their older white counterparts." In the end, only if Washington can pick itself up by the bootstraps—improve its schools and fund its police force—will African Americans, rich and poor, be inclined to take further risks on the city.

The most affluent African-American county in the United States is Prince George's County in Maryland, with African Americans making up over 60 percent of the population.

ROSA LEE

In 1994 the *Washington Post* published a series of stories by Leon Dash called "Rosa Lee's Story: Poverty and Survival in Washington."

For four days *Post* readers learned about Rosa Lee, an African-American woman who lived in one of Washington's poorest neighborhoods. A mother of eight children by six different men, dependent on welfare and addicted to drugs for a large part of her adult life, Rosa Lee did what she could "to support her family." She shoplifted on a regular basis, peddled heroin, and turned many of her children on to drugs.

In Dash's stories Rosa Lee is not portrayed as a villain. Rather, she is seen as a whole person—someone who was raised by a domineering mother, was illiterate (and therefore unable to obtain a decent job), and ultimately died of AIDS (acquired immune deficiency syndrome).

To read about Rosa Lee is to feel appalled at one moment and sympathetic the next—appalled when she spends her welfare check on drugs but sympathetic when she is brutally beaten by one of her husbands. Like many Washingtonians who live in poverty, Rosa Lee is neither entirely responsible for her circumstances nor entirely free from blame.

While many famous and powerful people work in Washington, D.C., the majority of the people who live there are often forgotten. In bringing to light the story of one poor African-American woman, Leon Dash helped others better appreciate the complicated problems that continue to face the urban poor.

ETHNIC WASHINGTON, D.C.

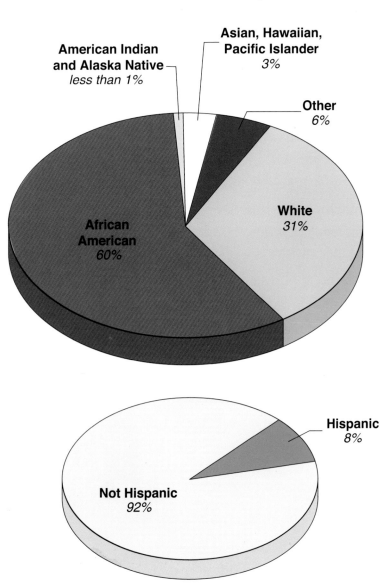

Asian, Hawaiian, Pacific Islander
3%

American Indian and Alaska Native
less than 1%

Other
6%

White
31%

African American
60%

Hispanic
8%

Not Hispanic
92%

Note: A person of Cuban, Mexican, Puerto Rican, South or Central American, or other Spanish culture or origin, regardless of race, is defined as Hispanic.

Since the early 1900s people of Hispanic descent have settled in the nation's capital. The Hispanic population received a big boost in the 1980s, when refugees from El Salvador fled that country's harsh right-wing regimes. These newcomers often settled in Mount Pleasant and Adams Morgan, and the community grew quickly as more and more Salvadorans followed in search of greater economic opportunity. Today, people of Hispanic descent continue to flock to the nation's capital from Central America.

Washington is also full of well-off people who are committed to living in the nation's capital, people who thrive on the pace, grit, and excitement that goes with living in an international city. The wealthiest, some of whose families have been living in the district for generations, generally live in the Spring Valley area, often on Foxhall Road. Most other middle- to upper-class people of all races have moved to the district to work for the federal government. Very well educated (there is a higher percentage of Ph.D.'s per capita in Washington than anywhere else in the world), members of this group, sometimes described as "government wonks," don't usually settle permanently in the district.

Washington, D.C.'s, Hispanic community is a culmination of peoples from many different Latin-American countries.

Overall, many Washingtonians are loyal to their city and are making an effort to bridge the racial divide. As one resident said, "I don't think there are black, white, or Hispanic potholes."

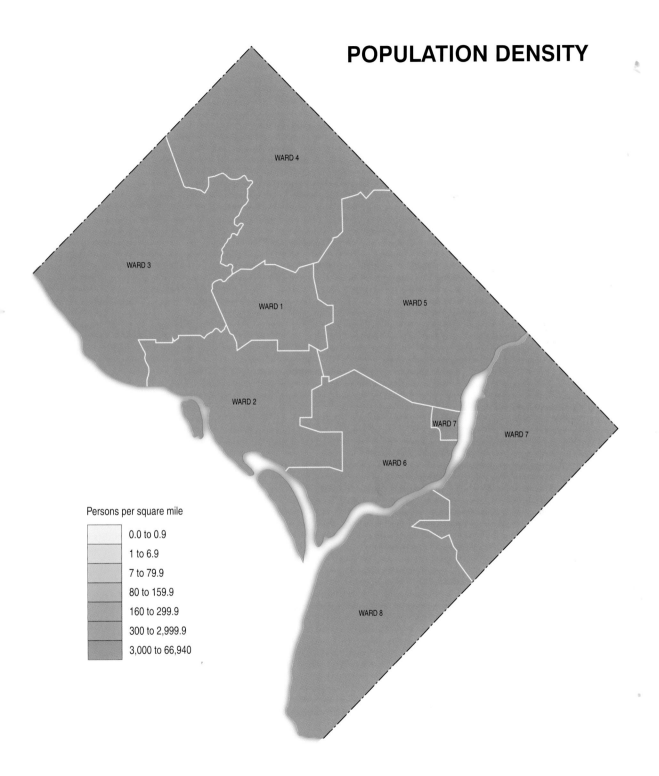

POPULATION DENSITY

WARD 4

WARD 3

WARD 1

WARD 5

WARD 2

WARD 7

WARD 7

WARD 6

WARD 8

Persons per square mile

- 0.0 to 0.9
- 1 to 6.9
- 7 to 79.9
- 80 to 159.9
- 160 to 299.9
- 300 to 2,999.9
- 3,000 to 66,940

Since the 1990s better city services have made the district a more desirable place to live. These improvements have coincided with a countrywide boom in real estate. "The cost of homes in the district has skyrocketed," said one resident. "The prices are insane."

The high prices have hurt low-income renters the hardest—usually black families that live in old, well-located houses that have been divided into apartments. Landlords looking to cash in, raise rents on these long-term

Over the five-year period of 2000 to 2005, real estate prices in Washington, D.C., rose by nearly 90 percent.

tenants, or simply evict them and sell the homes to developers for big profits. At the same time some African-American families lucky enough to own their homes have decided to sell. "We had to decide what to do," said one African American living downtown. "My childhood home was suddenly worth a mint. Do we stay or do we sell?"

Many have decided to sell. As a result, as richer African Americans flee the city for neighboring suburbs, they are leaving the lower class behind. At the same time such poorer areas as Petworth and Shaw—neighborhoods once considered dangerous—are now trendy. "If you told someone you were having dinner at 14th and P ten years ago," said a white Washington lawyer, "you would have been laughed at. Now it's the hottest neighborhood in town, complete with fancy shops, restaurants, and a Whole Foods [supermarket]."

As the city's fortunes have turned for the better, Mayor A. Anthony Williams has made a concentrated effort to bring young single people, families, and empty-nesters into the district. To that end the city has gone on an enormous building spree, tearing down hundreds of units of public housing and replacing them with mixed-income communities.

"The way it works is this," a Washington government employee said. "A third of the units are subsidized in part for working-class families, a third are subsidized more generously for the poor, and a third are for wealthier people at market rate. The goal is to get different people of different races and incomes living together."

Still, despite the real estate boom and the influx of young, usually white, professionals buying condos, Washington remains a Chocolate City at heart. "The perception in the district today is that Washington has gotten less black," said the journalist Marc Fisher. But he added, "In reality, the racial composition hasn't changed all that much. In the upcoming mayoral race [in 2006], all five candidates are black."

SENATE BEAN SOUP

The story goes that Fred Thomas Dubois, a senator from Idaho from 1901 to 1907, was such a bean soup fan that he forced a resolution through Congress requiring that it be on the Senate lunch menu every day. Other people give Senator Knute Nelson of Minnesota the credit for introducing bean soup to the congressional kitchen in 1903. Regardless of who introduced it, Senate bean soup is the hottest-selling dish in town. In fact, it is so popular that the Senate dining room makes it in 50-gallon batches—three times a week! Have an adult help you with this recipe.

2 pounds dried navy beans
1 pound smoked ham hocks
1 onion
butter
salt and pepper

Wash the beans in hot water until they are white. Put beans in 4 quarts of hot water. Add the ham hocks and boil slowly for approximately 3 hours in a covered pot.

Chop the onion and braise in butter. When the onion is a little brown, add to the soup. Season with salt and pepper.

THE ARTS

One problem Washington definitely does not have is a lack of things to do. Among the city's great strengths are its museums, monuments, parks, and historic sights. And that doesn't include its varied neighborhoods, its art, or its restaurants.

Many Washingtonians enjoy the fine art collections in their city; from the National Portrait Gallery to the Phillips Collection (a private museum of contemporary art), there is a lot to see. Washington's government buildings are also graced by much fine art. John Trumbull, an early American painter, created the beautiful *The Declaration of Independence, July 4, 1776* that hangs in the Capitol Rotunda. Also in the Capitol are bronze statues of Thomas Jefferson and Benjamin Franklin. As a local fireman put it, "There's art pretty much everywhere around here. You don't have to search too hard."

The National Statuary Hall in the Capitol, once the original House of Representatives chambers, now displays ninety-nine statues of notable persons from the United States.

There is also a thriving music scene in the district. The National Symphony Orchestra, which was founded in 1931, plays regularly at the John F. Kennedy Center for the Performing Arts. Then there's the U.S. Marine Band—a special Washington treat. Founded in 1798 by an act of Congress, this band has performed at every presidential inauguration since 1801. The group's most famous leader was John Philip Sousa, the March King, who composed such favorites as "The Stars and Stripes Forever."

SPORTS

Many Washingtonians have one important thing in common—adoration for the Washington Redskins football team that borders on insanity. There are other sports teams in the nation's capital as well. In the early 2000s the basketball great Michael Jordan came out of retirement to play for the Washington Wizards. Though "his Airness" couldn't deliver a championship, in 2002 the Wizards made it to the play-offs for the first time in years. Those with a taste for college basketball can follow Georgetown, which became a powerhouse under Coach John Thompson and has produced such NBA stars as Patrick Ewing and Alonzo Mourning. Washington also has a hockey team, named the Capitals. While no one could mistake the district for a hockey-crazed town like Montreal, the Capitals have a strong following. And now—some would say *finally*—Washington has a baseball team again. In 2005 the Montreal Expos moved to the district and became the Washington Nationals.

Still, Washington remains a football town. "Basketball and hockey are OK," one fan said, "but time stops around here for the Redskins. Football is the one thing that brings everyone in this city together."

The Washington Nationals currently play at Robert F. Kennedy Memorial Stadium.

THE REDSKINS

A tie that binds most Washingtonians together—regardless of race, religion, or wealth—is their football team, the Redskins. One die-hard fan remarked, "People here are nuts for the 'Skins. Absolutely, certifiably nuts!"

It's true—Washingtonians have stayed loyal to their team through good times and bad. The team is so popular that divorcing couples have asked the courts to divide their season tickets fairly. Their home games have been sold out for close to forty years, and there is a long waiting list for season tickets.

The good news for nonfans is that Sunday afternoons in the fall are the best times to shop. "That's when I buy my week's groceries," Sheila Cribbs, a mother of three, said. "Everyone else is at the stadium or parked in front of the TV."

In the early 2000s the Redskins fell on hard times. But in 2005 the owner Daniel Snyder brought back the beloved coach Joe Gibbs, and the team made the play-offs for the first time in years. "What can I say?" said one fan. "In Washington Joe Gibbs is practically a God."

Springtime brings Washingtonians downtown to the Mall to participate in a variety of festivals. The most famous is the Cherry Blossom Festival, celebrated each April to mark the beautiful blossoms on the cherry trees at the city's Tidal Basin. But many others are also worth keeping an eye out for.

"My favorite," said second grader Johnny True, "is the kite festival." Spring is marked in the district by hundreds of multicolored kites dipping and diving around and above the Washington Monument. In June and early July the contributions that different ethnic groups have made to our country are celebrated in the Smithsonian Folklife Festival. Set up on the Mall, the festival brings together an international array of people, food, arts, crafts, and exhibits. Though not technically a festival, the National Symphony Orchestra's open-air concerts give all Washingtonians a reason to take a picnic basket and blanket to the Capitol grounds and listen to beautiful music. A special treat takes place on July 4, when fireworks shoot up over the Washington Monument as the orchestra plays.

Fourth of July fireworks light up the Washington, D.C., sky.

THE PRESIDENTIAL INAUGURATION

No other city can boast an event as stirring as the presidential inauguration, a time every four years when the president is sworn in and addresses the nation. In 1933 Franklin Roosevelt told the country that was suffering from the ravages of the Great Depression, "The only thing we have to fear is fear itself." In 1961 John F. Kennedy implored the nation, "Ask not what your country can do for you; ask what you can do for your country."

The inauguration is also a time of great celebration. In 1993 Maya Angelou recited "On the Pulse of the Morning," a poem written especially for the occasion. Reportedly, President Bill Clinton attended fourteen formal balls on the day of his second inauguration. (When President Jackson was inaugurated back in 1829, he shocked the wealthier set by inviting his less-refined friends over to the White House.)

Chapter Four

A City in Transition

Washington, D.C., is an odd creature. From 1874 to 1973 the city was ruled by three commissioners appointed by the president and overseen by congressional committees. Even when Washington finally won the right to limited home rule in 1973 and was allowed to elect its own mayor and city council and to pass legislation, Congress had to approve its budget and could veto its laws. As one local reporter remarked, "For years Washington has been a ward of the federal government, which neglects it."

The district's first mayor of the modern era, Walter Washington, who served from 1975 to 1979, ran a fiscally sound administration. Unfortunately, Mayor Marion Barry Jr., who followed Washington in office, did not. The district became known as a city that could not provide basic services to its citizens. Luckily, the turn of the century brought better days to the nation's capital. Under the leadership of Mayor Anthony A. Williams, the people of Washington finally learned how to work with Congress to govern the district effectively.

The Supreme Court building was built as a symbol of "the national ideal of justice in the highest sphere of activity."

Washington, D.C., is the home of our federal government, which is divided into three branches: the executive (the president), the legislative (the Senate and the House of Representatives), and the judicial (the courts). Indeed, most American states and cities, including Washington, D.C., have a similar governing structure.

Executive Branch

Despite the influence of Congress, the mayor remains an influential figure. In Washington the mayor is elected to a four-year term, with no term limits. The mayor appoints heads of such departments as police and fire and submits a budget to the city council for a vote. The key player in the history of modern-day Washington has been the city's second mayor, Marion Barry Jr., who was first elected in 1978.

Barry was born in Itta Bena, Missouri, in 1936 and grew up in Memphis, Tennessee, in a poor family with seven sisters. A good student, Barry eventually found his way to LeMoyne College in South Memphis, where he became active in student government and the civil rights movement. In his senior year he took part in a Memphis bus desegregation case.

In 1960 he became a head of a new civil rights organization called the Student Nonviolent Coordinating Committee and addressed that year's National Democratic Presidential Convention. He told the delegates, "For 350 years the American Negro has been sent to the back door in education, housing, employment, and the rights of citizenship at the polls." These were bold words for a young man addressing a hall full of mostly white politicians.

Barry made his way to Washington, D.C., in 1965 and almost immediately organized an African-American boycott of a city bus line that was planning a fare increase. Hard on the heels of that victory, Barry became one of the leading advocates for home rule and was soon well known and respected in the district's African-American communities.

As mayor he initially earned the good-will of the entire city, including the wealthier whites, who saw in him a superb politician who might be able to get the city's spiraling budgets under control. But throughout the 1980s Barry, with no conservative opposition, championed a liberal philosophy in which the government provided jobs and services and paid little attention to the city's budget or physical condition.

In March 1996 Mayor Marion Barry Jr. gave a State of the District speech urging the city's residents to keep up their faith in the efforts being made to transform and revitalize their city.

Today, Barry admits that his emphasis may have been a bit off. "My focus was on social services, jobs, and education," he said. "In retrospect, we should have paid more attention to roads and bridges."

Either through lack of funds or poor management, under Barry's watch the quality of the city's social services continued to decline dramatically. Barry remained a popular mayor, however, throughout the 1980s, until he was convicted of drug possession. In what became a national embarrassment to the city, a videotape of Barry purchasing crack cocaine was broadcast to televisions throughout the country.

When his brief prison term was over, Barry went about the business of resurrecting his political career. Though he had lost the support of the white neighborhoods, he was still immensely popular in the lower-income African-American parts of the city. He moved into the African-American Ward 8, won a council seat, and in 1994 defeated the incumbent mayor, Sharon Pratt Kelly, in the Democratic primary. He then easily won the general election.

"What kind of citizenry would re-elect a mayor who went to jail for doing drugs?" one citizen asked. Another had a slightly more balanced view. "Mr. Barry is a tremendous politician," he said, "but he's a lot like nuclear power. On a good day, he can light the city. On a bad day, he can blow it up."

After completing his final term as mayor, Marion Barry Jr. did not drop out of D.C. politics. Instead, he got elected to the city council. Sadly, Barry has remained a prisoner of his addictions, even in his old age. In 2005 Barry tested positive for cocaine and was indicted for failing to file a tax return for five years straight. Further, it was discovered that the ex-mayor was hanging around a crack house near his home.

ANTHONY A. WILLIAMS

Born in 1951 Anthony A. Williams rose to power during Marion Barry Jr.'s final term. Williams was appointed by the congressional control board to serve as the district's chief financial officer after the district suffered years of fiscal mismanagement. When Williams led the city into a long over-due fiscal recovery, he was drafted to run for mayor in 1998.

"After years of Marion Barry Jr., D.C. residents were hungry for a less corrupt and more growth-oriented government," said the journalist Marc Fisher, "and chose a mayor who is very much an accountant and bureaucrat with no elective experience."

Known for always wearing a bow tie, Williams, an African American, has worked hard to balance the city's books. He has also done everything he can to spur development and to bring new businesses to the district. A prag-matic politician with a good relationship with Congress, he is largely credited with getting Washington back on track. "He may be a little bit bor-ing," said the writer Leslie Pillner, "but he is competent, and that's what Washington needs."

Under Williams's administration, city services like trash pickup have improved. Unsafe, poor neighborhoods have been redeveloped. Though some citizens say that he lacks passion—and some African Americans in the city complain that he is too focused on issues that concern whites, such as business development—most Washingtonians agree that Anthony A. Williams has been a good mayor.

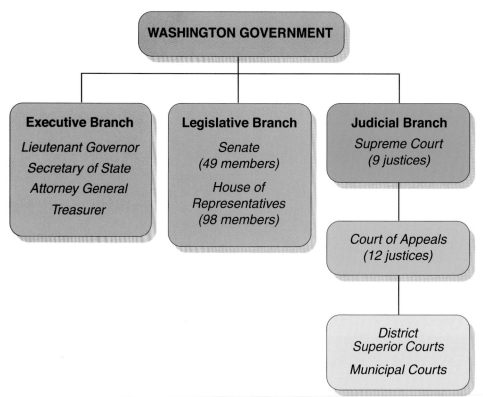

WASHINGTON GOVERNMENT

Executive Branch
Lieutenant Governor
Secretary of State
Attorney General
Treasurer

Legislative Branch
Senate
(49 members)
House of Representatives
(98 members)

Judicial Branch
Supreme Court
(9 justices)

Court of Appeals
(12 justices)

District Superior Courts
Municipal Courts

The Legislative Branch

Washington is divided into eight wards, each of which elects one member to the city council. Five additional councilpeople are elected "at large" in a city-wide vote. The city council gets the first crack at the mayor's budget each year, before sending it along to Congress.

Judicial Branch

The district has two levels of courts. The lower level, called the Superior Court, is broken into several different divisions that include family, criminal, civil, and housing courts. The highest court in the district is the Court of Appeals. All judges in Washington are chosen by the president, who picks from a list of three names given to him by a local judicial appointment commission. All judges serve for fifteen-year terms and are usually reappointed.

IMPROVING CITY SERVICES

In the 1980s and 1990s Washington's ability to provide basic services, such as garbage collection, declined. For example, the winter of 1995 brought record blizzards to Washington, but days passed before streets were plowed. "I live right across the border in Takoma, Maryland," Skip Aronson, a journalist, said. "The streets on the Washington side were covered with snow, while ours were plowed pretty much right away." Though part of the problem was that Washington, a southern town, was not equipped to deal with so much snow, the main issue was its poor economic situation. "Local plowing companies refused to work for the city of Washington," one native said. "They were afraid they may never get paid." Over the past eight years city services have improved dramatically. "It's simple," said a local fireman. "The richer folks moving into town weren't going to stand for trash on the front steps of their new condos."

A Washington, D.C., street remained unplowed after the blizzard of 1996.

Indeed, people simply demanded better services. Still, without the right mayor, the angry cries of an unhappy citizenry would have done very little to change how the city was run. In 1998 the people were smart enough to vote into office someone as disgusted with business as usual in the district as they were. "Tony Williams got into office to keep taxes down and to make sure the trains run on time, basic things ignored by previous mayors," said a D.C. journalist. Under Williams's watch, Washington has transformed into a city where snow is plowed and the trash is picked up.

CRIME

Despite Washington's improvement in providing basic services, crime remains a serious problem in the district's poorer, largely African-American, neighborhoods. Thirteen-year-old Markeisha Richardson said, "We had two people shot in my building once. And the other day some boys jumped out of a car and started shooting. They looked younger than me. I just don't know why life is so crazy sometimes."

In the 1980s Washington was dubbed Murder Capital USA. Crack cocaine, the drug of choice in poor neighborhoods across the country in the late 1980s and early 1990s, contributed greatly to Washington's soaring crime rate. With drugs come drug dealers and drug gangs fighting and often dying for turf.

Since then, due to the efforts of Police Chief Charles Ramsey, the overall rate of violent crime throughout the city is down. But while the wealthier neighborhoods experience little crime, the poorer sections in the eastern part of the city remain problematic. In April 2005 the *Washington Post* ran a story about a mother named Shandra Smith, whose anxiety typifies that of many poor parents, often African American, as they do what they can to keep their children safe. In 1993 Smith's two older children, a law-abiding son and daughter, were shot to death in a case of mistaken identity by a drug gang. Today, Smith worries about her two younger boys, Charles and Marquis, now teenagers. "When my big kids were killed," Smith said, "I looked at my little kids and I thought, 'One day they'll be teenagers, too. . . . I have to protect the ones I have left. '" In an effort to do that, Smith moved her two surviving sons to a new neighborhood near Eighth and H streets. But it wasn't long before she discovered that her new neighborhood was the home of Murder, Inc., a violent drug gang. Though Smith's boys are fine, they are worried, too. "I don't want to die," Charles recited in a poem at church, "for who would carry out the trash? . . . I don't want to die, for who will protect my family?"

Indeed, one of Washington's continuing, stubborn problems is what to do about the continuing drug trade and the violence that goes with it. Even so, out-of-towners should not be afraid of visiting. "I've lived here for twenty years," said Neil Feinburg, a Washington stockbroker. "And the threat of crime doesn't cross my mind especially." Though crime has encouraged some residents, especially those in poorer neighborhoods, to leave town for the suburbs, many Washingtonians remain happy right where they are. Ivan Reik, a construction worker, remarked, "The district has good neighborhoods and bad neighborhoods. Sure, there's crime, but don't forget that most of Washington is pretty beautiful."

Police patrol high-crime neighborhoods in Washington, D.C.

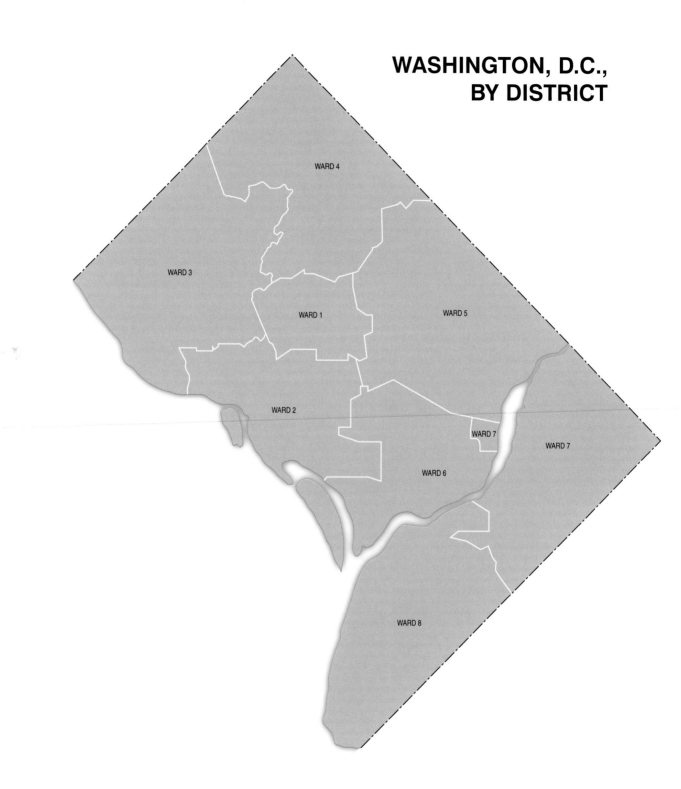

WASHINGTON, D.C., BY DISTRICT

WARD 4

WARD 3

WARD 1

WARD 5

WARD 2

WARD 7

WARD 7

WARD 6

WARD 8

CELL PHONES

Like many cities, Washington has to adjust to changing times to keep its citizens safe. In 2004 the district passed a law that required drivers to use hands-free devices when talking on cell phones. But police still come across hundreds of motorists zooming down Washington streets, holding their phones to their ears. "I see it every day," Master Patrol Officer Fred Rosario told the *Washington Post*. "They give me every excuse in the book." Some tell police they didn't know about the law. Some say they only need to chat with their children. "People are going to do what they think they can get away with," said Lieutenant Byron Hope, a traffic safety coordinator. Overseeing dangerous cell phone use may not be as exciting as stopping a robbery. On the other hand, stopping a traffic accident before it happens is a smart way to make sure the people of Washington stay safe.

GIVING PUBLIC SCHOOLS A NEW CHARTER

Besides crime, Washington's other major problem is its public schools. Indeed, many Washington schools are overcrowded or downright unsafe. Typically, Democrats have favored education policies that give more money to the schools to be used for smaller classes and better facilities. But with the Washington schools in such disarray, the city has turned to a solution traditionally associated with the Republican party: charter schools.

The mission of Washington, D.C.'s, public schools is "to develop inspired learners who excel academically and socially in . . . schools that instill confidence and . . . enthusiasm."

A charter school is a public school that's run by a private entity, not the city. In brief, a private business approaches the city with a plan to run a certain kind of public school, for instance one that will focus on the arts. The city government then approves that plan and lets the business set up its school using public money. Initially, the Democratic Mayor Williams was against the idea. But then he had a change of heart. He said that he "got up one morning and decided there are a lot of kids getting a [bad] education, and we could do better."

So far the charter-school experiment has reduced the rolls of public schools from 85,000 to 58,000 students. Still, its results have been mixed. "The good ones are terrific," said the journalist Marc Fisher. "The bad ones should've been closed the day they opened."

By all accounts, one of the best is the Cesar Chavez School, where students focus on learning about government. Another success story is the SEED School, which received Harvard University's "Innovations in American Government Award."

Despite the mixed results, Washington's school superintendent, Clifford Janey, is interested in using the charter model to fix the city's still-underperforming public schools. Janey wants to "rebrand" certain high schools. In April 2006 he suggested changing Eastern High School's name to D.C. Latin and modeling the school after the famous Boston institution. The new school would focus on teaching foreign languages and the humanities. Other public schools would focus on different subjects. "High school should be the crowning experience for young people," Janey told the *Washington Post*. "We want to identify high schools with particular brands."

Along with charters, Washington has also experimented with a voucher program in which certain poor families are given money by

A school voucher rally takes place outside the Supreme Court building.

the government to send their children to a private or parochial school. With only one thousand students participating, it's hard to tell how well it is working. But one thing is clear—before it can be considered a truly great city, the elected officials and people of Washington need to keep working together to make their school system better.

LOOKING AHEAD

Unquestionably, Washington, D.C., has made enormous strides over the past eight years. The district has become a safer, cleaner place to live. City services have improved dramatically. Though there is still work to be done, primarily in crime prevention and education, the citizens of Washington have a right to be proud and to hope that even better days are ahead. On the district Web page, Mayor Anthony A. Williams put his hopes for the city like this: "My vision for the district is a simple vision, but one that is shared by citizens from Anacostia to Adams Morgan—from Southeast to Northwest. Our citizens deserve to live in the best city in America. We are, after all, the nation's capital."

Chapter Five

Work in the Nation's Capital

Since the 1870s when Boss Shepherd led a drive to modernize the city, the federal government has been a stable employer in the nation's capital. Indeed, most of the city's population works for the government or serves the people who do. But while Washington's economy has been bolstered by the federal government, the city's budget has proved almost impossible to manage. The reasons for this have to do with the city's unique relationship with Congress. Most Washingtonians would agree that when Congress granted the district home rule, it imposed what *The New York Times* called "a bad financial and political deal on the city." According to former Mayor Barry, "Those of us who were fighting for home rule were so anxious to get some degree of freedom, we didn't examine what it was. We inherited a mess."

ECONOMIC WOES IN THE DISTRICT

There are many obstacles that make governing Washington successfully next to impossible. The city is not allowed to tax commuters who

In Washington, D.C., the government is the largest employer with a variety of jobs at federal and local levels.

81

make up two-thirds of the district's workforce. It cannot tax the 43 percent of the property within its borders that is owned by the government, diplomatic missions, or nonprofit institutions. The city must pay for a variety of "safety-net" social service programs like Medicaid, the cost of which it splits with the federal government. (Most other cities pay nothing for Medicaid.) In 1974 the district's Medicaid bill was around $17 million. Today, thirty years later, that number has ballooned to well over $200 million!

Add into the mix the fact that Washington is a government town. Hundreds of thousands of people are employed by the U.S. government in jobs ranging from president to trash collector. Most people move to Washington to work for the federal government, making it difficult for the city to attract small businesses. Once a business leaves the city limits for Maryland or Virginia, it is a complete financial loss to the district. James Gibson, the city's planning commissioner, explained, "If you move out of New York [City] to Westchester County [a suburb, also in New York state] you still pay taxes to the state, which kicks back some to the city of New York in the form of state aid. Here, if you move, it's a 100 percent loss to Washington."

Washington's efforts throughout the years to level the playing field have largely failed. One of the city's main gripes has always been the lack of a commuter tax. But the reporter Frank Clines said, "To pass a commuter tax would need the cooperation of Congress, and Congress just picks on Washington. And there's no way that Virginia and Maryland would let it pass." Though it's hard to blame the senators of Washington's border states for wanting to spare their citizens another tax, this impasse has deprived the district of a vital source of income that every other major city in the country takes for granted.

The Bureau of Engraving and Printing offers employment opportunities from administrative support and security specialists to chemists and engineers.

(Because of Washington's inability to tax commuters, the city does have a high restaurant tax of 10 percent—still not enough to balance its books.) Fred Cooke, the city's former chief lawyer, remarked, "I think you could bring the smartest person from the Harvard School of Government down here, and he couldn't make this thing work."

The revenue generated by taxing the half million people who commute into Washington, D.C., every day would contribute to city services and upkeep. However, the U.S. Supreme Court rejected an appeal to allow the tax.

WASHINGTON, D.C., WORKFORCE

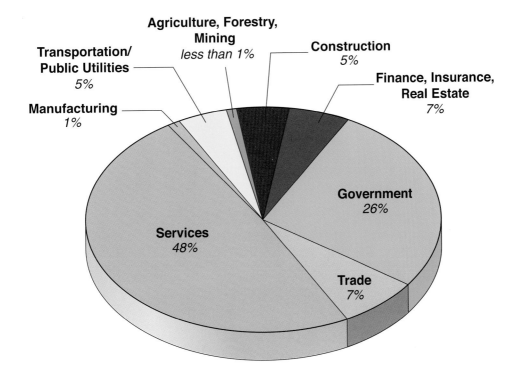

Agriculture, Forestry, Mining
less than 1%

Construction
5%

Transportation/
Public Utilities
5%

Finance, Insurance,
Real Estate
7%

Manufacturing
1%

Government
26%

Services
48%

Trade
7%

BALANCING THE CITY'S BOOKS

Though some citizens accuse Mayor Williams of being too focused on development, there is little doubt that he has helped make the city more attractive to businesses. "After years of red ink, we have a balanced budget," said Randall Militello, a policeman. "It's hard to believe."

Some of it has to do with good timing. Starting in the late 1980s a boom in the high tech industry brought many jobs to neighboring Virginia. Some of that money has spilled over into Washington. Wealthier people moved into the city, building up the tax base.

With real estate values booming, the city has been able to increase property taxes and turn the deficit into a small surplus. Recently, the city's bond rating has been upgraded, and Congress has approved budgets for the city that include millions of dollars in money earmarked for a variety of programs.

The real estate market in Washington, D.C., remained active during July 2005.

Of course, having more money is a large part of what has enabled Mayor Williams to improve city services. Garbage pickup, snow removal, pothole repair, and general infrastructure maintenance have all improved in the last eight years. "It's great for me," said Richard Miles, a father of two young children. "The parks and playgrounds are in much better shape."

SMOKE-FREE WASHINGTON

In April 2006 Washington joined other cities in enforcing a tough new no-smoking law. From now on district residents are not allowed to smoke in such public places as restaurants, offices, and apartment building lobbies.

Business owners objected, complaining that the ban would drive customers to Virginia, where public smoking is still legal. Supporting their view was Mayor Williams, who refused to sign the initial bill after it was passed with a veto-proof majority by the city council. Always probusiness, Williams said the new law went too far in limiting where people could eat and work.

Still, those Washingtonians interested in public health won out, and the law took effect. Recent studies have shown that smoking bans haven't hurt businesses as much as was feared. "I love it," said the D.C.-based writer Marc Temple. "It's nice to go to a restaurant without having to breathe in the fumes of someone's disgusting cigarette."

2004 GROSS DISTRICT PRODUCT: $77 Million

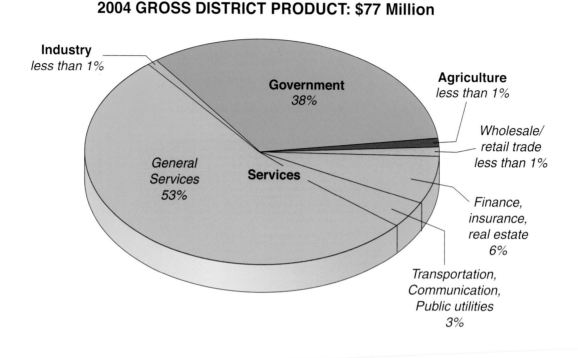

Industry
less than 1%

Government
38%

Agriculture
less than 1%

General
Services
53%

Services

Wholesale/
retail trade
less than 1%

Finance,
insurance,
real estate
6%

Transportation,
Communication,
Public utilities
3%

DEVELOPMENT AND THE STADIUM

"No doubt about it," said the writer Leslie Pillner, "Mayor Williams is going to be remembered for his obsession with development."

A pragmatic politician, Mayor Williams has prided himself on being able to work with a Republican Congress and business leaders to bring new businesses and housing to the district. Though helped by a booming economy and soaring real estate prices, Williams's success rate is still impressive. Under his watch, new housing has been built in poor neighborhoods—housing that has attracted new stores and restaurants. But while many Washingtonians applaud Williams's ability to bring new business to the city, some members of the African-American community think he is focusing on the affluent at the expense of the community.

However, Williams is quick to defend his record. In April 2005 he addressed a conference at the Harvard Kennedy School:

> *There are three cities in D.C.: the international, the federal, and the local. People always ask me why I spend so much time with the ambassadors that come through. To them, I say, "Chill." If these ambassadors go back to their countries and say, "Great city, great people," they'll want to invest.*

Still, not all Washingtonians are believers. The conflict between the mayor and large segments of the African-American community intensified in the fight over America's great pastime: baseball.

For many years the district had a baseball team. The Washington Senators won the World Series in 1924 behind the arm of Walter Johnson, one of the greatest pitchers in major-league history. But in 1969 with fan interest dwindling, the Senators moved to Seattle. Since that time many Washingtonians have wanted baseball back. In 2005 they got their chance, when the Montreal Expos were looking for a new home. Mayor Williams lured them to the district, in part by promising them a brand-new stadium. To help sell the idea to the city, Williams suggested that the stadium be constructed near the navy yard along the Anacostia River, generally thought to be a bad neighborhood. His hope was that a fancy new arena would spur business development and make life better for the largely poor people who live in the area. "On paper, its a great idea," said one resident. "I mean, baseball is great. The question is, who is going to pay for the stadium?"

Many African Americans don't want to foot the bill. After all, why should their tax dollars be used to pay for a sports arena that will be mostly used by whites? But Williams has stuck to his guns, pointing out that the stadium will not be built using tax dollars but by selling bonds. Further, he continues to assure Washington's African-American community that the new stadium will bring new business to the district. After several close votes on the city council, the new stadium was approved. The price tag, originally calculated at $475 million, has already shot up to $600 million. "The stadium is emblematic of Williams's governing philosophy," said the teacher Henry Greene. "Developing neighborhoods, building new housing to attract new business."

The Nationals currently play at RFK Stadium, however, their new home stadium is scheduled to open in spring 2008.

A STRING OF SUCCESSES

Yes, the numbers reflect good economic times, but as he finishes up his second term, Mayor Williams has a right to be happy. Since he took office in 1998, the District of Columbia has produced 59,000 new jobs, a 9.6 percent growth.

Williams also reinvested Washington's budget surplus in the city. In 2005 he earmarked $500 million for new programs and services. His budget funded day care for 1,200 children on the city waiting list and job training for eight hundred unemployed people. Williams has also been able to cut back on property taxes, saving each citizen an average of $200 a year. One resident, a lawyer, said, "Ten years ago no one would have thought we'd be where we are today."

Of course, like all big cities, Washington still faces a string of problems: unemployment, crime, and poor schools. As some people find jobs, there are always others who are left behind. And the rich get richer, many of the poor stay right where they are.

Still, Mayor Williams and the people of Washington have much to be happy about. It is up to Washington's citizens and the next mayor to build on the success of his administration. "We can't backslide," said the student Phyllis Hall. "The people of Washington are beginning to see just how good our city can be."

Mayor Anthony A. Williams supported Washington, D.C.'s, Human Support Services, such as day care, by proposing a 4.5 percent increase to the 2006 budget.

Chapter Six

A Monument to Our History

Washington, D.C., is a tourist's dream. Nowhere else in the United States is our country's heritage, its magnificence and tragedy, so gloriously on display. Though spring is the most beautiful time of year to visit, the district is a thrilling place during every season.

A WALK ALONG THE MALL

As one Washingtonian said, "The Mall has it all." Indeed, there are so many monuments, statues, and museums along this famous strip that it is impossible to do justice to them all. Here is a sample of some of the interesting spots a visitor shouldn't miss.

The Lincoln Memorial

At the head of a reflecting pool stands the famous memorial to Abraham Lincoln, the nation's sixteenth president, who led the United States safely through the Civil War. Soon after his assassination in 1865 a memorial was

Visitors await the opening of the Washington Monument to view the dramatic landscape of Washington, D.C.

Built to resemble a Greek temple, the Lincoln Memorial pays tribute to the nation's sixteenth president.

planned to honor his memory, but it was not until 1912 that the current site was chosen by Congress. Henry Bacon was selected to design the marble building, and the cornerstone was laid on the anniversary of Lincoln's birthday in 1915.

Sculpted by Daniel Chester French, the centerpiece of the memorial is a 19-foot statue of Lincoln sitting thoughtfully in a chair. To the left the words of the Gettysburg Address, delivered by Lincoln during the dedication of a cemetery near the end of the Civil War, are carved into the wall. On a mural above the address, the Angel of Truth frees a slave. To the right of Lincoln's statue are the words of his second inaugural address, delivered toward the end of the Civil War, in which he urged his countrymen, "With malice toward none, with charity for all, . . . to do all which may achieve and cherish a just and lasting peace among ourselves and with all nations."

Through the years, the Lincoln Memorial has been the site of many important historical events. Most notably, in 1963 Martin Luther King Jr. delivered his famous "I have a dream" speech from the steps of the monument.

The Vietnam Veterans Memorial

From the Revolutionary War to the Korean War, the American public usually believed in the causes for which they were asked to fight. The Vietnam War marked the first time a large portion of Americans felt we were in the wrong. During the late 1960s some young people burned their draft cards and marched for peace, and many political leaders spoke out against U.S. involvement in the conflict.

By the war's end in 1975, 58,000 Americans had died in Vietnam. A twenty-one-year-old Yale University student, Maya Ying Lin, designed a monument to honor these men and women. She decided that "the names would become the memorial." Although the Vietnam Veterans Memorial is simple—a series of black granite slabs with the name of every single soldier who died in the war carved in small letters—it conveys great emotion. Known now to many simply as the Wall, this deeply affecting memorial has become one of Washington's most popular since it opened in 1982.

The Washington Monument

Past a reflecting pool, the district's most famous landmark stands 555 feet high. First suggested in 1783 (the Founding Fathers' original idea was a simple statue of General Washington on his horse), the monument did not actually begin to take shape until 1848. The Civil War halted construction, and later work stopped again for lack of funds. (About 150 feet up the side of the memorial, it's easy to see where work was stopped by the slight difference in the color of the marble.) The

The Wall at the Vietnam Veteran's Memorial honors the more than 58,000 fallen soldiers of the Vietnam War.

monument was finally completed and opened to the public in 1888. Views from the top of the Washington Monument are extraordinary, but the lines to get there can be long!

The Jefferson Memorial

Thomas Jefferson was the author of the Declaration of Independence, secretary of state under George Washington, and our nation's third president. Though he died on July 4, 1826, exactly fifty years to the day after the adoption by Congress of his famous declaration, a memorial in his honor was not completed until April 13, 1943. Jefferson was also an architect with a fondness for domed structures (like his home in Monticello, Virginia), and his memorial is built in the same style. Words to some of Jefferson's most famous speeches are engraved on the walls inside the monument. Smack in the center of the dome is a 19-foot-tall bronze figure of Jefferson wearing a long fur-lined coat, knee pants, and buckled shoes.

Framed by Japanese cherry trees, the Jefferson Memorial is widely regarded as one of the prettiest spots in the city. "The view across the Tidal Basin to downtown Washington is gorgeous," John Crimmons, a longtime resident, said, "especially in the spring, when the cherry blossoms are in bloom. It's one of my favorite places on the planet."

The Thomas Jefferson Memorial, located in Washington, D.C.'s, Tidal Basin, was designed with Jefferson's architectural tastes in mind.

THE NATIONAL ARCHIVES

We hold these truths to be self-evident, that all men are created equal, that they are endowed by their Creator with certain unalienable Rights, that among these are Life, Liberty, and the pursuit of Happiness.

—Thomas Jefferson, the Declaration of Independence

Virtually no American child grows up without studying the Declaration of Independence, the U.S. Constitution, and the Bill of Rights, perhaps the three most important documents in our nation's history.

The original copies of these documents are kept in the new Rotunda for the Charters of Freedom at the National Archives. There you can see Thomas Jefferson's famous pronouncement to the world of the American colonies' decision to fight for their freedom from the British. At the bottom is John Hancock's famous signature!

All four pages of the Constitution are also on display, along with the signatures of the delegates to the Constitutional Convention in 1787. The Bill of Rights, which sets forth freedom of the press, speech, and worship, is also exhibited.

To keep these precious documents safe and to preserve them from deterioration, they are enclosed in specially designed cases.

PLACES TO SEE

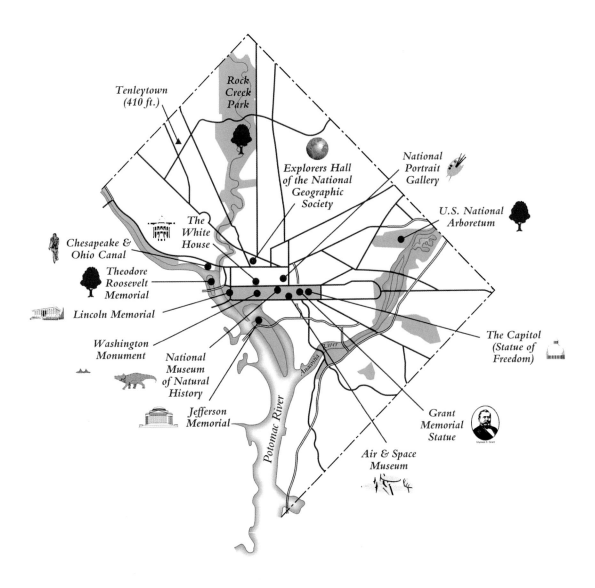

Tenleytown
(410 ft.)

Rock
Creek
Park

Explorers Hall
of the National
Geographic
Society

National
Portrait
Gallery

U.S. National
Arboretum

The
White
House

Chesapeake &
Ohio Canal

Theodore
Roosevelt
Memorial

Lincoln Memorial

Washington
Monument

National
Museum
of Natural
History

Jefferson
Memorial

Anacostia River

The Capitol
(Statue of
Freedom)

Grant
Memorial
Statue

Ulysses S. Grant

Air & Space
Museum

Potomac River

Take a walk along the Mall, and you are likely to see some interesting-looking buildings. Is that a Greek temple? a medieval castle? Actually, these buildings are part of perhaps the most impressive string of museums in the country, if not the world. The Smithsonian Institution was established in 1846, when an English scientist named James Smithson left a large sum of money to the U.S. government to found an organization devoted to increasing knowledge. Today, Smithson's legacy has been turned into a series of fascinating museums that every family member can enjoy. "And what is great," said Barbara Eyman, a Washington lawyer, "is that they are free!"

There's not enough room to list all of the museums that are part of the Smithsonian, here are a few that shouldn't be missed.

The National Air and Space Museum

Have you ever wondered what the Wright brothers' first airplane looked like? Well, it's on display here, along with the *Spirit of St. Louis*, the plane that Charles Lindbergh piloted on the first nonstop solo trip across the Atlantic Ocean on May 20–21, 1927. (It took him more than 33 hours, which was considered fast traveling in those days.)

The museum also holds the *Friendship 7* space capsule, the first ship to orbit the earth, and Skylab, the first space station, as well as a genuine moon rock. Also thrilling are the IMAX films about space and air travel shown on screens so large, you get the feeling that you are flying yourself.

The National Museum of American History

Perhaps the first thing you'll notice in the front entrance of this museum is the Foucault pendulum, which swings slowly back and forth, never stopping. Each time it knocks down one of the red markers that surround it in a circle, it gives proof that the earth is rotating.

At the National Air and Space Museum, some of the planes that shaped the world of commercial air travel are on display.

But this museum is mainly devoted to collecting odd artifacts of American history. Various things are here—from the ruby slippers Dorothy wore in *The Wizard of Oz* to a display of gowns worn by our nation's first ladies. Perhaps, best of all is the floor devoted to automobiles—everything from the earliest Model T to the fanciest sports car. There are also old bicycles, trains, and rooms full of model ships.

The National Museum of Natural History

"I looked up, and there it was. An absolutely giant elephant. Very cool," said Brenda Childs, a fifth grader from Arlington, Virginia. Indeed, a single step into the Museum of Natural History gets you into the swing of things.

Standing in the main lobby is a 13-foot-tall, 8-ton African bush elephant.

And there's more inside—eighty-one million artifacts documenting the planet's history and the natural environment—everything from reassembled dinosaur skeletons to the 45.5-carat Hope Diamond, one of the largest blue diamonds in the world. Also exciting is the newly remodeled O. Orkin Insect Zoo, which includes displays on the evolution of insects and a giant collection of bugs. Children can crawl through a 14-foot model of an African termite house, and there is a giant beehive (safely behind glass), not to mention live cockroaches and leaf-cutter ants. "It's one of my favorite places to take the kids," said Rachel Hill, a Washington mother. "I've just got to make sure they don't bring any of the live exhibits home!"

Visitors to the Smithsonian Museum of Natural History are greeted by a huge stuffed African elephant.

THE CHERRY BLOSSOM FESTIVAL

Perhaps Washington's most beautiful sight is the annual blooming of its cherry trees. The lovely trees were donated to the United States as a friendship gift by the mayor of Tokyo in 1912 to mark the "ephemeral nature of beauty." They bloom for about two weeks every spring.

The Cherry Blossom Festival Parade is usually slated for the first Saturday in April. But as one longtime D.C. resident said, "Depending on Mother Nature, the blossoms are sometimes either not out yet or already gone!" As a result, parties and ceremonies in honor of the cherry blossoms run from late March through early April.

Tourists flood the city during these weeks. During a special ceremony a three-hundred-year-old Japanese lantern is lit. This is followed by a speech on friendship by the Japanese ambassador and talks by representatives of the U.S. government.

Smart blossom-peepers use the Metro to get downtown to avoid the agony of finding a parking spot. And some tourists head to the Maryland suburbs, notably Kenwood, which has beautiful cherry blossoms of its own, but no crowds.

THE WHITE HOUSE

It's an odd fact that the only president who did not live in the White House was George Washington. The reason? It wasn't built. When John Adams moved in, in the year 1800, it was hardly the beautiful mansion it is today. The War of 1812 didn't help, either, as the mansion was burned by the British. It took several years of work before it was once again ready for occupation in 1817. As years have passed, the presidential mansion has been improved. In 1833 running water was added. Gaslights replaced oil lamps in 1849. Though historians are unsure, Millard Fillmore is credited with installing the first bathtub in 1851. No one disputes the fact that our twenty-seventh president, 340-pound William Howard Taft, had a custom-made tub installed that was large enough to fit four grown men.

The White House has 132 rooms—some of them famous, such as Lincoln's bedroom. Perhaps the most important is the Oval Office, where the president works. Much of the government's important business still takes place in the White House.

THE HOLOCAUST MEMORIAL MUSEUM

One of the district's most powerful sites, the Holocaust Memorial Museum, tells the story of the six million Jews and others who were killed by the Nazis between 1933 and 1945. Documenting the horrors of the Holocaust through photos, film, artifacts, and interactive exhibits, this museum is best viewed with a parent or school group. In one exhibit, "Daniel's Story: Remember the Children," you follow the life of Daniel and his family walking through rooms that show his home before the Nazis took power and learning how this boy was affected by the Holocaust. Open since 1993 the Holocaust Memorial Museum is one of the finest additions to the city.

The White House, home to every president since John Adams, has retained much of its exterior structure since 1800.

Washington is a city with plenty of places to go for a little dose of nature. "The Arboretum is so still and quiet," said Mary Neuwirth, an architect. "I go there to walk and unwind." With 444 acres of trees, flowers, and plants, the National Arboretum is a great place to relax and forget about the pressures of school or work. Like many areas in Washington, it is especially beautiful in the spring, when it is covered by azaleas. The rhododendron in the summer are lovely as well.

Smack in the middle of the city is Rock Creek Park, which covers nearly 2,000 acres of rolling hills, woods, and meadows. Although the park has over 15 miles of trails, you don't have to take a long hike to enjoy it. Many Washingtonians use it in the course of a normal business day. "It's great to be able to walk to work on a nice day through Rock Creek," said Frank Clines. "It's one of the things I really appreciate about living in this city." Rock Creek Park is especially nice on weekends, when its roads are closed to cars and joggers, and bikers and in-line skaters take over.

This survey of Washington's sites is by no means complete. There is the Library of Congress, the National Gallery of Art, the Navy Museum, the Hirshhorn Museum and Sculpture Garden, the National Museum of American Art, the National Portrait Gallery, the National Postal Museum, and the new National Museum of the Native-American Indian—the list is long. Come for a weekend and start looking. Or you can take the advice of Jeffrey Livingston, a D.C. security guard, who said, "It takes weeks to see everything here. If you really want to see it all, you've got to move here."

Bushes and trees blossom in the National Arboretum.

STARS & BARS: The Stars and Bars is the official symbol of the District of Columbia.

THE FLAG: Three red stars float above two red stripes against a white background on the District of Columbia flag. The design is based on George Washington's family coat of arms and was adopted in 1938.

THE SEAL: A woman who represents Justice places a wreath on a statue of George Washington. The national bird, a bald eagle, sits next to Justice. In the background the Capitol appears on the right, and the sun, proclaiming a new day, rises on the left. The seal was adopted in 1871.

District Survey

Established: President George Washington chose the site of the city in 1791. It became the nation's capital on December 1, 1800, when Congress moved in.

Origin of Name: Washington is named for the nation's first president, George Washington. The District of Columbia is named for the explorer Christopher Columbus.

Nickname: The Nation's Capital

Motto: Justice for All

Bird: Wood thrush

Flower: American beauty rose

Tree: Scarlet oak

Wood thrush

American beauty rose

WE SHALL OVERCOME

This simple yet moving hymn was the theme song of the civil rights movement of the 1960s. The hymn's roots are an old African-American church song, "I'll Overcome Some Day." It has been sung at rallies by thousands of voices and has echoed around the world in many languages. On August 28, 1963, over 200,000 people gathered on the Mall in Washington, D.C., to hear Martin Luther King Jr. deliver his famous "I have a dream" speech and to sing "We Shall Overcome."

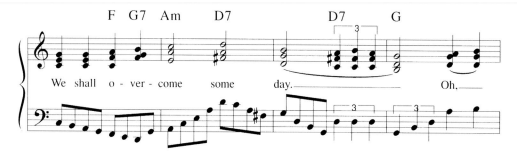

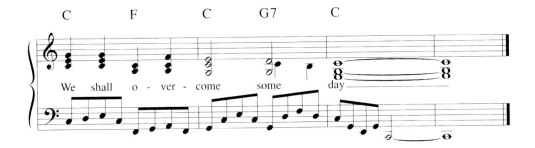

We are not afraid,
We are not afraid,
We are not afraid today,
Oh, deep in my heart, I do believe,
We shall overcome some day.

We are not alone . . . (today) . . .
The truth shall make us free . . . (some day) . . .
We'll walk hand in hand . . . (today) . . .
The Lord will see us through . . . (today)
Repeat first verse

Highest Point: 410 feet above sea level, at Tenleytown

Lowest Point: sea level, at the Potomac River

Area: 68.25 square miles

Greatest Distance North to South: 15 miles

Greatest Distance East to West: 14 miles

Bordering States: Maryland to the northwest, northeast, and southeast; Virginia to the southwest

Average January Temperature: 35ºF

Average July Temperature: 78.9ºF

Hottest Recorded Temperature: 106ºF on July 20, 1930

Coldest Recorded Temperature: −15ºF on February 11, 1899

Average Annual Precipitation: 50 inches

Major Rivers: Anacostia, Potomac

Bodies of Water: Tidal Basin of the Potomac River, Washington Channel

Trees: beech, black walnut, cedar of Lebanon, dogwood, elm, holly, linden, locust, Lombardy poplar, magnolia, maple, oriental plane, pine, pin oak, red oak, scarlet oak, spreading ginkgo, sycamore, willow

Animals: chipmunk, fox, frog, muskrat, opossum, rabbit, raccoon, squirrel, turtle, woodchuck

Chipmunk

Birds: Baltimore oriole, blue jay, chickadee, duck, heron, finch, mockingbird, pigeon, sparrow, starling, thrush, warbler, woodpecker

Fish: catfish, largemouth bass, pickerel, shad, striped bass, sunfish, walleyed pike

Endangered Animals: American peregrine falcon, bald eagle, Hays Spring amphipod

TIMELINE

Washington, D.C., History

c. 1600 Piscataway Indians live near the Potomac and Anacostia rivers in what is present-day Washington, D.C.

1634 English settlers, led by Leonard Calvert, build the first town along the Potomac River.

1751 City of Georgetown is established.

1776 The Declaration of Independence is signed on July 4.

1789 George Washington becomes the first president of the United States.

1791 Virginia and Maryland cede land for the creation of a federal district; George Washington chooses Pierre-Charles L'Enfant, a French engineer and architect, to design the nation's capital city.

Perigrine falcon

1793 George Washington lays the cornerstone for the U.S. Capitol.

1800 President John Adams and his family move into the White House.

1814 Admiral Sir George Cockburn orders British forces to burn the White House during the War of 1812.

1847 Congress returns to Virginia ceded land that is unnecessary for the federal government's use.

1848 Construction of the Washington Monument begins.

1861 Troops from New York's Seventh Regiment protect Washington, D.C., from the advancing Confederates during the Civil War.

1864 Battle of Fort Stevens, the only Civil War skirmish fought in Washington, takes place.

1865 Abraham Lincoln is assassinated by John Wilkes Booth at Ford's Theatre.

1867 Howard University is founded as an institution of higher learning for people of all races.

1874 Congress passes legislation taking away the right to elect a city government from D.C. citizens.

1888 Washington Monument opens to the public.

1901 Theodore Roosevelt prints the words "The White House" on his presidential stationery, making the name official.

1912 Japan sends a gift of three thousand flowering cherry trees to the United States to be planted in the nation's capital.

1919 In anti-Negro riots, mobs kill four African Americans and wound seventy.

1922 Lincoln Memorial is completed.

1943 Jefferson Memorial opens.

1944 Senator Theodore Bilbo proposes legislation to deport African-American D.C. citizens to Africa.

1963 Martin Luther King Jr. delivers "I have a dream" speech.

1964 Twenty-third Amendment to the Constitution grants D.C. citizens the right to vote in presidential elections.

1968 Riots break out in response to the assassination of Martin Luther King Jr.

c. 1970 Potomac River cleanup effort is successful, allowing fish to survive in the river.

1970 D.C. voters are allowed to elect a nonvoting delegate to the House of Representatives.

1973 Home rule is instituted, enabling D.C. voters to elect their own mayor and city council, with continued congressional oversight.

1978 Marion Barry Jr. is elected mayor of the district.

1990 Sharon Pratt Kelly becomes the first female mayor of Washington.

1994 Marion Barry is re-elected to his fourth term as mayor of Washington. The same year President Bill Clinton puts the city under the thumb of a congressional control board.

1998 Anthony A. Williams is elected mayor.

2001 Control board is abolished; on September 11 a hijacked plane crashes into the Pentagon, killing 189 people.

2005 Washington, D.C., announces that it has a budget surplus.

CALENDAR OF CELEBRATIONS

Presidential Inauguration Although this January event occurs only once every four years, it is a major celebration in the city. The newly elected president parades down Pennsylvania Avenue from the Capitol to the steps of the White House to take the oath of office. A festive parade with floats, bands from each state, and marching military unit passes by the president's reviewing stand.

Black History Month February is the month during which Washington, D.C., and all Americans pay tribute to the forward-thinking and courageous African Americans who have contributed so much to this country. Special events are held at the Smithsonian Institution and the Martin Luther King Jr. Library.

Black History Month

President's Day This holiday marks the birthday of both Abraham Lincoln and George Washington on the third Monday of February.

Cherry Blossom Festival A two-week-long festival marks the blossoming of the cherry trees along the Potomac River. This annual event celebrates the three thousand cherry trees given to the United States by Japan in 1912 to represent the two countries' friendship. In 1965, 3,800 more trees were accepted by First Lady, Lady Bird Johnson. The highlight of the celebration is the Cherry Blossom Festival Parade, which is usually held on the first Saturday in April.

Sakura Matsuri This annual April festival honors Japanese-American relations. It features artists, martial arts demonstrations, authentic Japanese cuisine, ikebana (flower-arranging) workshops, and children's activities, including origami and wood carving.

White House Easter Egg Roll On the Monday after Easter Sunday people flock to the grounds of the Ellipse, the pavilion in the park behind the White House, where one thousand wooden eggs are hidden. Entertainers, food, and contests enliven the day.

White House Easter Egg Roll

Smithsonian Kite Festival Every spring kite fliers gather at the Mall near the Washington Monument to enjoy a day of spectacular kite flying. Hundreds of colorful kites whip and wave around the monument.

Memorial Day Weekend This three-day event includes parades, wreath-laying ceremonies at the Tomb of the Unknown Soldier (across the Potomac in Arlington, Virginia), and the annual National Memorial Day Concert by the National Symphony Orchestra on the west lawn of the U.S. Capitol.

Smithsonian Folklife Festival See, hear, smell, taste, and look at the display of arts and crafts created by representatives of international, regional, and ethnic cultures at this lively weeklong event sponsored by the Smithsonian Institution. Songs, music, and dancing add to the entertainment every June on the Mall.

Independence Day The Fourth of July is a very special celebration in Washington, D.C. The day begins with a parade down Constitution Avenue, which is followed by entertainment and concerts throughout the day and evening. The grand finale is a spectacular fireworks display above the Washington Monument.

D.C. Blues Festival The finest blues singers and bands perform in Anacostia Park each summer at this free festival.

Adams Morgan Day On the first Sunday after Labor Day the residents of this multiethnic neighborhood hold a fair with dancing, music, food, and arts and crafts from Africa, Latin America, and the Caribbean.

National Christmas Tree Lighting The lighting of the National Christmas Tree by the president is part of the seasonal Pageant of Peace. Nightly musical programs cascade across the grounds of the Ellipse throughout the holiday season.

National Christmas Tree Lighting

Edward Albee (1928–   ) is a playwright who was born in Washington, D.C. His best-known work, *Who's Afraid of Virginia Woolf?*, was made into a popular movie starring Elizabeth Taylor and Richard Burton. Albee has won a Pulitzer Prize three times for his plays, *A Delicate Balance*, *Three Tall Women*, and *Seascape*.

Marion Barry Jr. (1936–   ), who was born in Itta Bena, Missouri, has long been active in the politics of Washington, D.C. He came to prominence for his work in downtown renewal during the 1970s. Barry was first elected mayor in 1978. He was re-elected twice, but then in the late 1980s he was convicted of drug possession. Even after serving a prison sentence, he remained popular and was again elected mayor and later city councilman.

Clara Barton (1821–1912) became known as the Angel of the Battlefield for her work tending to the wounded in Washington, D.C., during the Civil War. After the war she helped organize the American Red Cross, which provides aid in times of war and natural disaster.

Clara Barton

Elgin Baylor (1934–   ) was one of basketball's great forwards. Born in Washington, D.C., he played for the Minneapolis and Los Angeles Lakers.

Alexander Graham Bell (1847–1922), who moved to Washington, D.C., in 1879, is best remembered for inventing the telephone. A man of many talents, he had a lifelong interest in helping the deaf and hard of hearing. From 1896 to 1904 he was president of the Washington-based National Geographic Society.

Frances Hodgson Burnett (1849–1924) built a house in Washington, D.C., with proceeds from her successful book and play *Little Lord Fauntleroy*. Today she is best known for her book *The Secret Garden*, which has been adapted for stage and film.

Connie Chung (1946–   ) is a Washington-born journalist. She has anchored several television news shows, including *News at Sunrise* and *Saturday Night with Connie Chung*.

John Foster Dulles (1888–1959) was secretary of state during the administration of Dwight D. Eisenhower. It has been said that this position was in his blood: his grandfather John W. Foster and his uncle Robert Lansing had both served as secretaries of state. Dulles was born in Washington, D.C.

Connie Chung

Edward Kennedy "Duke" Ellington (1899–1974), the Washington-born and trained jazzman extraordinaire, was a pianist, orchestra leader, and composer. Ellington left a legacy of popular songs, such as "Mood Indigo," as well as longer concert works.

Duke Ellington

Katharine Graham (1917–2001) became president of the *Washington Post* in 1963. She championed aggressive investigative reporting of the sort made famous by the reporters Carl Bernstein and Robert Woodward, who broke the story of the Watergate break-in scandal during President Richard Nixon's term in office. They earned a Pulitzer Prize for the *Post*.

Goldie Hawn (1945–   ) was born in Washington, D.C., and attended American University before she giggled her way to stardom on television's *Laugh-In*. She won an Academy Award in 1969 for Best Supporting Actress in *Cactus Flower* and went on to star in such films as *Private Benjamin* and *The First Wives Club*.

Helen Hayes (1900–1993) was born in Washington, D.C. She was an actress known as the First Lady of the American Theater, although she was also popular on screen, radio, and television. She won her first Academy Award in 1931 and landed another Oscar for *Airport* in 1970. The Helen Hayes Award for artistic achievement in professional theater has been established in her hometown of Washington, D.C.

J. Edgar Hoover (1895–1972) was a lawyer and criminologist who served as the director of the Federal Bureau of Investigation. He is credited with turning the FBI into a fully professional organization during his forty-eight years of service. Hoover was born in Washington, D.C.

William Hurt (1950–   ) is an actor who won an Oscar in 1985 for his role in *The Kiss of the Spider Woman.* His many film credits include *The Big Chill* and *Children of a Lesser God.* The son of a career diplomat, Hurt was born in Washington, D.C.

William Hurt

Noor al-Hussein, Queen of Jordan (1951–   ) was born Lisa Najeeb Halaby in Washington, D.C. She went to school in the United States and graduated from Princeton University in 1974. In 1978 she married King Hussein of Jordan. As queen of Jordan she directs projects on education, government, women's development, environmental protection, social welfare, and international understanding.

Walter Johnson (1887–1946) was one of baseball's greatest pitchers. Although he was born in Kansas, he played for the Washington Senators from 1907 to 1927. Nicknamed the "Big Train" because of the speed of his pitching, Johnson was one of the five original inductees into the Baseball Hall of Fame.

Francis Scott Key (1779–1843) wrote the words to the national anthem, "The Star-Spangled Banner," after watching the British bombard Fort McHenry. Though born in Baltimore, he later lived in Washington, D.C., where he served as district attorney from 1833 to 1841. A park in Georgetown marks the site where his house once stood.

Francis Scott Key

Toni Morrison (1931–   ), the author of many books, including *Song of Solomon*, was born in Ohio and came to Washington, D.C., to attend Howard University. After graduation she taught at Howard and joined a local writers' group. Morrison has received every major literary award, including the Nobel Prize for Literature.

Roger Mudd (1928–   ) has worked as a reporter and newscaster for CBS and NBC. Mudd is respected for his knowledge of political affairs in his hometown of Washington, D.C.

Eleanor Holmes Norton (1937–   ) was born in the District of Columbia and has lived there for most of her life. She is a lawyer who has specialized in cases involving human rights and freedom of speech. Norton formed the National Black Feminist Organization and has taught at Georgetown University School of Law. A longtime nonvoting delegate to the House of Representatives, she was the first African-American congresswoman for the District of Columbia.

Chita Rivera (1933–   ) was born Dolores Conchita Figueroa del Rivero in Washington, D.C. A popular dancer and actress, she has starred in Broadway musicals such as *West Side Story* and *Bye Bye Birdie*. In 1984 she won a Tony award for her role in *The Rink*.

Leonard Rose (1918–1984), born in Washington, D.C., started studying the cello at age ten. He played with the Cleveland and New York City symphony orchestras from 1938 to 1951. He has taught cello at two of the leading music schools in the country—Julliard School of Music in New York and Curtis Institute of Music in Philadelphia. The concert cellist Yo-Yo Ma is one of his most successful and acclaimed students.

John Philip Sousa (1854–1932) was a Washington-born composer and musician who in 1880 became the bandmaster for the United States Marine Band. Known as the March King, Sousa went on to form his own celebrated band. He wrote comic operas, songs, suites, and more than one hundred marches including "The Stars and Stripes Forever" and "Semper Fidelis."

Walt Whitman (1819–1892) is one of America's most celebrated poets. He was born in New York but spent the Civil War years as a nurse's aide in Washington, D.C. His best-known works include a volume of poetry, *Leaves of Grass*, and "O Captain! My Captain!," a poem that mourns Abraham Lincoln's death.

TOUR THE DISTRICT

The White House All the presidents of the United States, except George Washington, have lived in the White House. The grand mansion, its cornerstone laid in 1792, is the oldest public building in Washington, D.C. More than one million visitors tour the White House each year. The president's office and private living quarters are not open to public view. Tours are limited to prearranged groups.

The U.S. Capitol Congress conducts its business in this huge, domed building. Several architects and engineers—beginning with William Thornton and including Benjamin Henry Latrobe, Charles Bulfinch, E.S. Hallet, and Thomas U. Walter—developed and built the U.S. Capitol. The building's 10-ton bronze main doors portray highlights of the life of Christopher Columbus. With its majestic dome and columns, the look of the Capitol has been re-created in many state-houses across the nation.

Washington Monument Built in honor of the nation's first president, this 555-foot white marble obelisk is circled by the flags of each state in the nation. An elevator takes visitors to the top for a panoramic view of the city.

Lincoln Memorial The Lincoln Memorial is an inspirational structure built to honor one of America's greatest presidents. Inside is a huge statue sculpted by Daniel Chester French, which shows Abraham Lincoln sitting in a thoughtful pose. Selections of Lincoln's famous speeches, including the Gettysburg Address, are engraved in the walls.

Jefferson Memorial A majestic 19-foot bronze statue of Thomas Jefferson stands inside this domed building with columns circling it. Excerpts of Jefferson's speeches decorate its marble walls.

Jefferson Memorial

Vietnam Veterans Memorial Bold and moving, this memorial of black granite rises out of the ground between the Washington Monument and the Lincoln Memorial. The names of all the Americans who died in the Vietnam War are carved into its stone panels. This creative memorial was designed by a young Yale University architecture student, Maya Ying Lin. Nearby is a statue of two women and a wounded soldier made by sculptor Glenna Goodacre that honors the women who served in the military during the Vietnam War. Also nearby is Frederic Hart's sculpture, "Three Fighting Men."

National Archives This museum contains the great treasures of the United States: the Declaration of Independence, the Constitution, and the Bill of Rights. The archives also features murals depicting scenes of America's early history, the signing of historic treaties and documents, and photographs of Washington, D.C.

The Castle Red stone towers rise above this medieval-style structure, which is the headquarters for the Smithsonian Institution. Inside is the tomb of James Smithson, whose bequest was used to found the Smithsonian.

National Air and Space Museum Here you can learn all about airplanes and aerospace technology. Special exhibits include the Wright brothers' plane, flown at Kitty Hawk; Charles Lindbergh's *The Spirit of St. Louis*; and the *Friendship 7* space capsule.

National Gallery of Art This museum displays paintings, sculpture, and decorative arts from throughout the history of western art. Be sure to stand in the center court of the East Building to watch the Alexander Calder mobile move.

Smithsonian Castle

National Museum of African Art This museum, which is completely underground, contains one the world's best collections of ancient and modern African art and artifacts. Highlights include textiles and carved ivory.

Arthur M. Sackler Gallery This collection contains masterpieces of ancient and modern Asian art. Chinese carved jade and lacquer, Southeast Asian stone and bronze sculptures, paper scrolls and paintings, and a rare collection of Persian miniatures are some of the treasures housed in this museum.

National Museum of Women in the Arts This museum celebrates the contributions of women artists from the Renaissance to the present. Painters in the permanent collection include Mary Cassatt, Georgia O'Keeffe, and Helen Frankenthaler.

Hirshhorn Museum and Sculpture Garden This round building is filled with contemporary art from the nineteenth and twentieth centuries. The museum is noted for the outdoor sculpture garden.

U.S. Department of the Interior Museum Visitors come to this museum to get a historical view of the American West and to see displays of Native American artifacts.

Ford's Theatre This theater has been restored to look as it did when President Abraham Lincoln was shot there by John Wilkes Booth. The basement museum houses exhibits about the assassination, including the pistol used by Booth and the flag that was draped over Lincoln's coffin.

Frederick Douglass Memorial Home You can visit the last home of Frederick Douglass, who is often referred to as the father of the civil rights movement. The house is decorated with furnishings from Douglass' time period. The home contains his vast library, including gifts from President Abraham Lincoln and the author Harriet Beecher Stowe.

Mary McLeod Bethune Council House Mary McLeod Bethune, an African-American educator and women's rights advocate, advised President Franklin Roosevelt. Documents that trace the development of the black women's movement are housed in this museum, which was the headquarters of the National Council of Negro Women, an organization founded by Bethune.

Anacostia Museum and Center for African-American History and Culture This new museum honors African-American history with varied exhibitions on significant historical events and the achievements of great black Americans. It also has displays about the Anacostia neighborhood where it is located.

Washington National Cathedral This huge Gothic cathedral—one of the world's largest—is renowned for its brilliant stained glass windows. The cathedral tower contains fifty-three bells, which ring every Sunday afternoon. You can attend a workshop there to learn to make a brass plate rubbing of medieval figures.

Washington National Cathedral

Dumbarton Oaks This splendid mansion, with its expansive grounds and gardens, is a quiet and restful place in the middle of the hustle and bustle of the city. Its museum contains an outstanding collection of Byzantine and pre-Columbian art.

John F. Kennedy Center for the Performing Arts A living memorial to the late president, this versatile arts center provides space for all kinds of performing arts. You can see plays, operas, ballets, musicals, and symphony and popular concerts.

U.S. Holocaust Memorial Museum This museum houses exhibits that honor the six million Jews and others who were murdered by the Nazis. A special exhibit presents events of the time from a child's point of view.

Library of Congress This is the biggest library in the world, but it contains more than just books. For instance, you can see the world's largest collection of comic books, as well as Pierre-Charles L'Enfant's original designs for the city of Washington, D.C. Recent renovations have brightened the brilliant marble staircases, murals, and mosaics.

Federal Bureau of Investigation Here you can learn about crime investigation methods and fingerprint techniques and see a live firearms demonstration.

National Aquarium You can see more than one thousand aquatic species at the aquarium. Be sure not to miss the shark and piranha feedings.

Bureau of Engraving and Printing Here you can watch money being printed. The printed money rolls off the presses in large sheets and is then cut into individual bills. This bureau manufactures currency, postage stamps, and special White House invitations.

Albert Einstein Statue You can climb into the lap of this great scientist. Maybe you can hear the universe spinning in his head.

National Zoological Park The highlights of this zoo are the famous panda bear Mei Xian, a gift from the Chinese government, and her son, Tai Shan.

FUN FACTS

George Washington oversaw the construction of the White House, but he never actually lived in it.

It is illegal in Washington, D.C., to build a structure taller than the Capitol.

Find Out More

Want to know more about Washington, D.C.? Check a library or book-store for these titles:

BOOKS

Bluestone, Carol. *Washington, D.C.—Guidebook for Kids*. Washington, D.C.: Noodle Press, 2003.

Connors, Jill. *Growing Up in Washington, D.C.: An Oral History*. Mount Pleasant, SC: Arcadia Publishing, 2001.

Finamore, Frank J. *Washington, D.C. Trivia Fact Book*. New York: Gramercy, 2001.

Landphair, Ted and Carol Highsmith. *Washington, D.C.* New York: Crescent, 2000.

VIDEO

Finley-Holiday Film Corp. *Washington, D.C.: City Out of Wilderness, the Definitive History*, 2005.

WEB SITES

The District
http://www.thedistrict.com
A complete online guide of everything happening in Washington.

Welcome to Washington, District of Columbia

http://www.dc.gov

The homepage for the city, which provides links to every aspect of city government.

Washington D.C., The American Experience

http://www.washington.org.

A site filled with articles and information about the district.

Smithsonian National Zoological Park

http://nationalzoo.si.edu/default.cfm

At this site explore the animals that live at the zoo, as well as learn about the zoo's mission in animal care, science, and education.

National Gallery of Art

http://www.nga.gov/

Learn about the Gallery's permanent art collection, take part in its weekly Web tour, while exploring its exhibitions, programs and events, and kid's page

Index

Page numbers in **boldface** are illustrations and charts.

ABOUT THE AUTHOR

Dan Elish is the author of many novels and nonfiction books for young readers. For Benchmark he has written about the Trail of Tears, Edmund Hillary, the state of Vermont, and Theodore Roosevelt. Dan lives in New York City with his wife and two young children.